AND HOW THEY ARE USED

POULTRY	MEAT	VEGETABLES		SALADS
Stuffings	Liver Chopped meat Ragouts Stews Meat pies Meat sauces	Cauliflower Onions	Tomatoes	Greens ...ato ...e-slaw
Fricassee Parboiling	Pot roast Stews			

	Roast pork
	Liver
	Kidneys
		Broccoli
		Brussels
		  sprouts
		Cabbage
			Red
			  cabbage
			Potatoes
				Tips of
				fresh, leaves
				with greens

Broiled chicken
Most chicken
  dishes
Stuffings
	Stews
	Gravies
	With butter
	  on steak
		Artichoke
		  hearts
		Beets
		Broccoli
			Carrots
			Celery
			Eggplant
				Greens
				Potato

	Hamburger Sauces	Cabbage Carrots Celery	Peas Potatoes	Greens Potato

	Broiled
	  chops
	Many meats
	Some veal
	  dishes
		Avocado
		Beans
		Beets
			Eggplant
			Parsnips
			Potatoes
				Cucumber
				Potato
				Many
				  others

Duck Turkey Stuffings	Marinades Roasts Stews Sausages Sauces	Brussels sprouts Cabbage Eggplant Limas Mushrooms	Peas Potatoes Spinach String beans Tomatoes Zucchini	Greens

Marinades	Marinades
	Lamb
	Stews
	Stuffings
	Spanish, Italian,
	  and Mexican
	  dishes
		Broccoli
		Mushrooms
		Zucchini		

Almost
  all
	Marinades
	Stews
		Chopped
		  on almost
		  all
				Greens
				Potato
				Vegetable

Stuffings	Lamb marinade
	Pork
	Roast lamb
	Roast veal
	Stuffings
		Beans: baked,
		  lima, soy,
		  string
		Eggplant
			Spinach
			Zucchini
			Boiled
			  potatoes	

Fresh with
  duck and
  geese
Stuffings
	Head cheese
	Pork
	Roasts
	Stews
	Sausage
	Stuffings
		Cabbage
		Carrots
		Fresh with
		  string
		  beans		

Almost all
  poultry
  dishes
	Stews
	Most
	  meat
	  dishes
		Cabbage
		Green
		  pepper
		Mushrooms
			Peas
			Tomatoes
				Greens
				Tomato
				Vegetable

Stuffings	Marinades
	Roasts
	Stews
	Croquettes
	Meat loaf
		Brussels
		  sprouts
		Cabbage
		Carrots
		Peas
			Squash
			Sweet
			  potatoes
			Sliced raw
			  tomatoes
				Fresh in
				  green
				  salads

Erna Laura Wolford Bixler
bought from Marion Powers
Monday afternoon, August 21, 1978
in beautiful Laramie, Wyoming

THE SUMMER COOKBOOK

Books by the Same Author

CASSEROLE MAGIC

CASSEROLE TREASURY

✤ THE
SUMMER COOKBOOK

By Lousene Rousseau Brunner

HARPER & ROW, PUBLISHERS, NEW YORK and LONDON

CONTENTS

PREFACE

SUMMER cooking presents problems to the family cook that do not exist in ordinary weather. Who wants to spend hours in a hot kitchen on a broiling summer day? Nevertheless, we may get just as hungry then as we do on cool days, and meals must be forthcoming.

Every recipe in this cookbook has been selected either to make cool and pleasant eating on hot days or to save the cook hours of toil in a hot kitchen, as well as to suggest dishes that should be welcome in spite of the heat. Many of the hot dishes included—and after all they can't be entirely eliminated for the season—can be prepared largely or wholly in the morning and refrigerated until time for them to go into the oven. It would be monotonous as well as expensive to rely wholly on chops and steaks all summer. Then too, there are many molded salads and desserts that can be made early in the day, as well as a considerable number of main dishes.

In order to cut down kitchen time for the cook, short cuts are suggested wherever possible without detriment to the quality of the dish, and frequent use is made of canned and frozen items. A brief section highlights the ever-more-popular back-yard cooking and picnic planning.

In the principal sections of this cookbook suggestions are offered for what to serve with the dishes described. Here the aim is to balance the meal. Nutritionists and dietitians warn us that a summer diet of all cold food is unwise, and therefore at least one hot item is included for each such recommendation.

LOUSENE ROUSSEAU BRUNNER

Wilton, Connecticut
November 1965

✤ COLD SOUPS

Cold soups are not so widely used in hot weather in this country as they should be. Here is an assortment of delightful cold soups, some jellied and some not. The soups offered here are varied in kind, including a number of unusual fruit soups, and they are easy to make.

COLD AVOCADO SOUP

3 avocados
2 cups lightly seasoned chicken stock
1 cup heavy cream

Pinch chili powder
1 teaspoon grated onion
Salt and pepper
Whipped cream

1. Peel and cut up 2 of the avocados, mash with a silver fork, and put in the top of a double boiler. Add the stock and heat to the boiling point.
2. Stir in the cream, chili powder, and onion and chill for several hours.
3. Season the cold soup and stir in the third avocado, peeled and cut in dice.
4. Ladle into individual plates, bowls, or cups and top each serving with a tablespoon of lightly salted whipped cream. *Serves 4.*

AVOCADO-CRABMEAT SOUP

1 cup coarsely chopped avocado
2 cups cooked crabmeat, canned, fresh, or frozen
¼ cup butter or margarine
¼ cup flour
1 teaspoon salt

Dash fresh-ground pepper
½ teaspoon dry mustard
4 cups milk or 2 cups top milk and 2 cups chicken broth
2 tablespoons minced onion
½ cup minced celery
Chopped chives

THIS is a rich but refreshing soup, and makes a delicious meal with only hot rolls and a tossed green salad to accompany it.
1. Melt the butter and blend in the flour, salt, pepper, and mustard. Gradually stir in the liquid or liquids, and cook until smooth and thick, stirring constantly.
2. Combine and blend in the remaining ingredients except chives, and chill.
3. Pour into a chilled bowl, and garnish with chopped chives. *Serves 5–6.*

Note: This soup can be made much faster by reducing the milk or chicken broth by ½ cup and blending everything in a blender with a cup of chipped ice. Serve at once.

WINE CONSOMMÉ

To 4 cups beef consommé add 1 cup dry red wine and 1 tablespoon lemon juice, seasoning to taste with salt and pepper. Serve either very hot or poured over ice cubes in old-fashioned glasses. *Serves 5–6.*

COLD BEEF CONSOMMÉ

3 cans condensed consommé
1 cup whipping cream
Salt to taste
Few drops garlic juice

¼ teaspoon monosodium glutamate (MSG)
1½ tablespoons lemon juice, or to taste
1 cup chipped ice

2

PUT all the ingredients in a blender except the ice, blend ½ minute, add the ice, and blend 20 seconds more. Pour into chilled cups or glasses. Serve at once. *Serves 5–6.*

BEEF BROTH ON THE ROCKS

PUT 3–4 ice cubes in old-fashioned glass. Pour beef broth over and garnish with lemon slice and sprig of parsley.

INSTANT BLENDER BORSCHT

2 cups dairy sour cream
1-inch slice of lemon, peeled
½ teaspoon salt

½ small onion, sliced
1 cup diced cooked beets (canned will do)
1 cup crushed ice

PUT 1½ cups of the sour cream in the blender, with the lemon, salt, onion, and beets. Cover and blend on high 15 seconds. Add the ice, cover, and blend 10 seconds longer. Pour into chilled soup cups or plates at once, and top each serving with a little of the remaining sour cream for a garnish. *Serves 4.*

FRUIT SOUP

½ cup peeled, sliced peaches
½ cup strawberries
½ cup cut-up rhubarb
½ cup orange sections
½ cup cut-up fresh pineapple

¾ cup sugar
½ teaspoon salt
2 whole cloves
2 tablespoons lemon juice
2 quarts water

MIX and chop all the fruits. Put in a saucepan and add remaining ingredients. Bring slowly to a boil, lower heat at once, and simmer 15 minutes. Rub through a sieve, put through a food mill, or remove cloves, put in a blender, and blend 20 seconds, covered. Chill well. *Serves 8.*

GAZPACHO SOUP

1 clove garlic mashed	1 large green pepper shredded
½ teaspoon paprika	1 small white onion sliced very thin
¼ cup olive oil	2 cucumbers diced or sliced
3 tablespoons wine vinegar	Salt to taste
6 cups cold water	Small chunks dry French or
3 ripe tomatoes peeled and	Italian bread
chopped	

THIS is a classic Spanish soup, though there are almost as many ways of making it as there are Spanish and Portuguese regions. This is a typical recipe.

Mix the ingredients in a large wooden bowl, in the order given. Mix well after each addition. At the end drop the chunks of bread on top and chill the soup thoroughly. Serve very cold. *Serves 8.*

Note: A pleasant variation is to substitute strong chicken broth for half of the water, and add lemon juice to taste.

CAVIAR MADRILÈNE

2 cans jellied madrilène soup at	½ teaspoon Worcestershire sauce
room temperature	Red caviar
1 tablespoon lemon juice	Dairy sour cream
1 teaspoon grated onion	Chopped chives
2 tablespoons sherry	

POUR the warm soup into a bowl and stir in the lemon juice, onion, sherry, and Worcestershire sauce. Pour into 4 soup cups and chill until almost set. At this point stir 1 teaspoon red caviar into each cup and chill until set. When ready to serve top each cup with 1 tablespoon sour cream, and sprinkle the cream with chopped chives. *Serves 4.*

Note: Some brands of madrilène do not jell well. If you use such a brand, dissolve a little plain gelatin in ½ cup of the soup, heat until gelatin is dissolved, and stir in.

4

JELLIED MUSHROOM SOUP

1 pound mushrooms chopped	1-2 tablespoons lemon juice
3½ cups chicken stock	1 envelope plain gelatin
2 tablespoons sherry	¼ cup cold water
Salt and pepper to taste	Dairy sour cream

1. Simmer the mushrooms in the chicken stock for 30 minutes. Strain through a food mill or coarse sieve, pushing as much of the mushroom pulp through as possible, or put in a blender and blend 15 seconds. Measure and add enough additional stock to make 3¾ cups.
2. Stir in sherry, salt and pepper and lemon juice to taste.
3. Soften the gelatin in the water. Bring the soup to a boil and stir in the gelatin, stirring until dissolved. Cool and chill well.
4. Serve in chilled cups with a scant tablespoon of sour cream as a topping. *Serves 4.*

POLISH BLACKBERRY SOUP

1 pint ripe blackberries well washed	2 cloves
	½ cup sugar
2 small lemons sliced thin	2 cups cold water
1-inch piece stick cinnamon	2 cups dairy sour cream

PUT all the ingredients except the sour cream into a soup kettle and bring to a boil. Lower the heat and simmer 10 minutes, or until fruit is soft. Remove cinnamon and cloves. Rub through a fine sieve or put in a blender and blend 20 seconds. Cool and chill well. Stir in sour cream before serving. *Serves 4.*

COLD RASPBERRY SOUP

4 cups ripe raspberries	½ bottle chilled dry white wine
½ cup sugar or to taste	1 cup water

SAVE out a few good berries for garnish and put the rest through a food mill or put them in a blender and blend 20 seconds. Combine with remaining ingredients, chill well, and serve with a few berries floating in each plate. *Serves 4–5.*

CHILLED SEAFOOD BISQUE

1 can condensed clam chowder
⅔ cup water
¼ cup chopped onion

1 cup flaked lobster or crabmeat,
or half of each, cooked, canned,
or frozen
⅔ cup light cream

1. Combine the soup, water, and onion, and simmer, covered, 5 minutes. Force through a sieve or put in a blender and blend 30 seconds.
2. Stir in the lobster or crab and cream and mix well. Chill thoroughly. Serve with a garnish of minced chives or parsley, or a few small shrimp. *Serves 4.*

COLD PINK STRAWBERRY SOUP RAINBOW ROOM

1 pound fresh ripe strawberries
1 cup water
1 bottle port wine
4 tablespoons sugar

Juice of 1 lemon
Pinch of salt
3 tablespoons arrowroot or flour
Light cream

1. Bring slowly to a boil the berries, water, and port wine, reserving a bit of the latter to blend with the arrowroot or flour.
2. Stir in the sugar, lemon juice, and salt and simmer a few moments.
3. Blend the arrowroot or flour with the reserved port wine and stir into the soup. Allow the soup to come barely to a boil. Remove from the heat, cool, and chill well.
4. Serve with a pitcher of light cream to be poured over the soup. *Serves 6.*

COLD SENEGALESE SOUP

3½ cups strong chicken stock
1 cup minced cooked chicken
1-2 teaspoons curry powder, to
taste

4 egg yolks, beaten
2 cups light cream
Shredded cooked chicken

1. Bring the stock to a boil and add the minced chicken and curry powder.
2. Stir a little of the hot stock ino the egg yolks and blend in the cream. Add this mixture to the soup and heat over very low heat until it thickens slightly, but do not let it boil. Cool and chill well.
3. Before serving check the seasoning and garnish each serving with a few shreds of chicken. *Serves 6–8.*

VICHYSSOISE GOURMET

8 leeks
3 large potatoes peeled and diced
small
¼ pound sweet butter melted
Hot water

1 quart hot chicken stock
Salt and pepper to taste
½ pint heavy cream
Chopped chives

1. Cut off the green part and tough outer leaves of the leeks. Split them into quarters and wash thoroughly to remove sand. Dry them, chop fine, and cook slowly in the butter.
2. Add the diced potatoes, and enough hot chicken stock to barely cover them. Continue to cook until potatoes are soft. Season to taste.
3. Put into a blender and add the remaining chicken stock as you blend the mixture.
4. At this point you can cool and chill the mixture, or you can add to the blender a cup of chopped ice, blend about 10 seconds more, and serve at once.
5. Sprinkle ½ teaspoon chopped chives on each bowl or plate. *Serves 6–8.*

COLD SOUP MIXTURES
(To be chilled thoroughly)

1. 1 can condensed black bean soup
    1 can condensed consommé
    1 can water
    1½ tablespoons sherry
    1 tablespoon lemon juice
    Thin slices of lemon to float on each serving. *Serves 4-5.*
2. 1 can condensed cream of chicken soup
    1 can condensed cream of mushroom soup
    1 can milk
    ½ can water
    1 tablespoon lemon juice
    1 cup cooked chicken diced small. *Serves 5-6.*
3. 1 can condensed green pea soup
    1 can condensed tomato soup
    2 cans ice water
    1 teaspoon curry powder, or to taste
    Sour cream for garnishing each serving. *Serves 6.*
4. 1 can condensed cream of chicken soup
    1 can cold milk
    Chopped parsley or chives for topping. *Serves 2-3.*
5. 1 can condensed tomato soup chilled
    1 can ice water
    2 teaspoons fresh basil chopped, or 1 teaspoon dried. *Serves 2-3.*
6. 1 can condensed pea soup
    1 can green turtle soup
    2 tablespoons sherry
    1 tablespoon dairy sour cream to top each serving. *Serves 4.*

✤ SANDWICHES

Any weather is sandwich weather, but probably summer is the time when most sandwiches are made—soup and sandwiches for luncheons and Sunday-night suppers, and sandwiches for picnics, as well as for snacks. Here is a collection of both hot and cold sandwiches just a little out of the ordinary.

COLD SANDWICHES

CHICKEN-CHEESE CLUB SANDWICHES

8 tablespoons cottage cheese
2 tablespoons chopped pecans
1 tablespoon chopped dates
9 slices white bread, buttered

Sliced chicken breast
Mayonnaise
Lettuce leaves
Sliced smoked tongue

1. Combine cheese, pecans, and dates and spread on 3 slices buttered bread.
2. Lay second slice buttered bread on top and cover with sliced chicken, a little mayonnaise, lettuce, tongue, and more lettuce.
3. Lay a third slice of buttered bread, buttered side down, on top to close the sandwich.
4. Cut the 3 sandwiches in triangles or quarters. *Serves 3.*

CURRIED CREAM CHEESE SANDWICH FILLING

3-ounce package cream cheese
6 pitted ripe olives chopped
¼ teaspoon curry powder, or to
 taste

1 teaspoon chopped chives
Oatmeal bread

MASH ingredients together and spread on 4 slices bread. Cover with additional slices. *Serves 4.*

COLD SANDWICHES   9

CREAM-CHEESE-BACON SANDWICH FILLING

3 slices bacon cooked crisp and
crumbled
3-ounce package cream cheese
¼ cup grated Parmesan cheese

½ teaspoon Worcestershire sauce
2 tablespoons light cream
¾ teaspoon chopped parsley or
chives

BLEND well and use as sandwich filling. *4 sandwiches.*

HORSERADISH CREAM CHEESE SANDWICHES

2 three-ounce packages cream
cheese
¼ cup dairy sour cream

2-4 tablespoons prepared grated
horseradish
Chopped parsley or chives
Salt and pepper to taste

BLEND ingredients well and make sandwiches. *6 sandwiches.*

EGG AND WATERCRESS SANDWICHES

½ cup finely chopped watercress
(stems removed)
½ cup coarsely chopped walnuts
4 ounces cream cheese

2 hard-cooked eggs sieved
Salt to taste
Thin slices of white or nut bread
Butter or mayonnaise

1. Mix the filling ingredients gently but thoroughly.
2. Spread the bread with butter or mayonnaise, then with the filling, cover with more buttered bread, trim off the crusts, and chill an hour or so. *1 cup of filling.*

NUT BREAD SANDWICHES

CUT the nut bread in very thin slices. Spread 1 slice with softened cream cheese mixed with a little cream, top with a second slice, spread it with more cream cheese, and place a third slice on top. Wrap the sandwiches in wax paper or foil and chill briefly.

TONGUE SANDWICH FILLING

1 cup minced cold cooked tongue   ½ teaspoon Worcestershire sauce
¼ cup thinly sliced stuffed olives   3 tablespoons mayonnaise

MIX and spread. *Makes 4 large sandwiches.*

HERO OR SUBMARINE SANDWICHES

THESE sandwiches, so popular nowadays with young and old, can make use of almost anything on hand.

Cut a round loaf of French bread crosswise into 2 circles, or split a long loaf of French or Italian bread lengthwise and spread both halves with butter or margarine, mayonnaise, or garlic or mustard butter, and pile on as many of the following items as your fancy dictates:

MEATS: Salami, bologna, spiced or boiled ham, prosciutto ham, liverwurst, sliced tongue, cold roast beef, cooked chicken or turkey

CHEESE: Swiss, Muenster, Cheddar, mozzarella, bleu, or any other

FISH: Tuna salad, sardines, anchovies, crab or lobster salad

MISCELLANEOUS: Thick-sliced tomatoes, crisp lettuce, chopped parsley, thin-sliced onions, green pepper rings, hard-cooked eggs, cole slaw, etc.

When the sandwich is loaded with as much as it can take, cover with the top layer, skewer together, cut in individual portions, wrap in aluminum foil, and chill 1–2 hours.

VARIETIES OF SANDWICH FILLINGS

MEAT: ham—tongue—cold roast beef—cold roast lamb—cold cuts
SALADS: Tuna—crab—salmon—lobster—egg—chicken or turkey
BREADS: White—rye—whole wheat—oatmeal—nut bread—sesame-seed bread—pumpernickel

CHEESE: All cheeses, including cream cheese
MIXTURES: grated carrot and mayonnaise—cream cheese, chopped olives, and mayonnaise—cream cheese and chopped dates—cream cheese and jelly—cream cheese and chopped nuts—baked beans and chili sauce or chopped pickle and mayonnaise—crumbled bacon and chopped hard-cooked egg and mayonnaise—chopped hard-cooked egg, sardine, and mayonnaise—peanut butter and crisp hot bacon—sardine and mustard butter and mayonnaise—cucumber and mayonnaise—red caviar and cream cheese—tomato, cheese, and bacon—cold meat and sliced cheese—ground ham and chopped pickle—cream cheese and chives or parsley—smoked salmon and cream cheese—smoked salmon and chopped egg—chicken chopped with preserved ginger or coconut—cream cheese and chopped chutney—chicken or turkey and thin slices avocado and mayonnaise—turkey, tomato, and sliced hard-cooked eggs—baked ham, Swiss cheese, and sliced dill pickle—turkey, tongue, and Swiss cheese on rye—watercress mixed with butter and a little grated onion.

HOT SANDWICHES

BROILED BEEF SANDWICHES

1½ pounds ground top round
1 loaf Vienna bread, unsliced
Soft butter or margarine
½ cup grated or finely ground onion

1 tablespoon Worcestershire sauce
1¼ teaspoons salt

1. Split the Vienna loaf lengthwise, and spread both halves with butter or margarine.
2. Mix together lightly but thoroughly the beef, onion, Worcestershire sauce, and salt and pile on the two half loaves, extending the filling clear to all edges. It should be about ½ inch thick.
3. Broil the half loaves about 15 minutes, 6 inches from the heat. Cut in serving portions when done. *Serves 8.*

BAKED CHEESE AND HAM SANDWICHES

1. Butter enough slices of bread (crusts removed) to cover the bottom of a shallow casserole or pie plate, fitted neatly together.
2. Cover this bread layer with fairly thick slices of Cheddar or American cheese, fitting them together.
3. Spread over the cheese a large—4½-ounce—can of deviled ham.
4. Cover this layer with another layer of bread slices, buttered side up.
5. For a 4½-slice bread layer, beat 3 eggs with 2 cups of milk and a little salt. Pour over the casserole gently. Sprinkle thickly with grated Parmesan cheese and paprika.
6. Let stand an hour or so in the refrigerator if possible, and bake 45–60 minutes in a 350° oven, or until a knife inserted in the center comes out clean. *Serves 4–6.*

BAKED LOBSTER-CHEESE SANDWICH

1 cup coarsely chopped lobster (6-ounce can)
½ cup Swiss cheese cut in small dice
¼ cup mayonnaise
2 tablespoons minced onion or shallots

½ teaspoon salt
1 teaspoon tarragon vinegar
4 hamburger buns or 8 slices white bread
Butter or margarine

1. Break up the lobster carefully, removing all bits of cartilage.
2. Combine lobster, cheese, mayonnaise, onion, salt, and vinegar.
3. Split and butter the buns or the bread and pile the lobster mixture on the bottom halves.

Cover with the top halves, wrap each sandwich in a square of aluminum foil, lay on a baking sheet, and bake 20 minutes in a 350° oven. Cool 2–3 minutes after removing from the oven, unwrap, and serve warm. *Serves 4.*

SWISS BAKED EGG SANDWICHES

6 slices white or oatmeal bread,
   crusts removed
Butter or margarine
¼ pound fresh mushrooms sliced
1 cup grated Swiss cheese

6 eggs
½ cup light cream
½ teaspoon salt
¼ teaspoon pepper
Paprika

1. Toast the bread lightly on one side and butter the untoasted side. Spread in a large shallow casserole, buttered side up.
2. Sauté the mushrooms lightly in 1 tablespoon butter or margarine and spread them over the buttered side of bread.
3. Sprinkle 1 tablespoon of the cheese on the mushrooms, and make a depression in the center of each slice of bread with the back of a tablespoon.
4. Break an egg into the center of each slice of bread.
5. Combine the cream and salt and pepper and pour gently over the eggs.
6. Sprinkle the rest of the cheese evenly over the eggs, dust the top with paprika, and bake about 20 minutes in a 350° oven, or until the eggs are set and the cheese is golden. *Serves 6.*

PUFFED CHEESE OPEN SANDWICHES

1 cup grated American cheese
2 egg whites beaten stiff
1 teaspoon Worcestershire sauce

½ teaspoon paprika
½ teaspoon dry mustard
4 slices white bread

BLEND ingredients except bread until smooth. Toast bread on 1 side. Spread the cheese mixture on the untoasted side and broil a few moments, until the cheese is puffed and brown. Serve hot. *4 servings.*

HAM–BAKED-BEAN TOASTWICH

1 small can baked beans (not with
   tomato sauce)
4½-ounce can deviled ham
1 tablespoon horseradish

½ cup minced celery
8 slices oatmeal or whole wheat
   bread

1. Mix all filling ingredients well and spread on half the bread slices. Cover with the remaining slices.
2. Lay the sandwiches on a baking sheet and bake 15 minutes in a 350° oven; or spread the sandwiches, top and bottom, with softened butter or margarine and brown slowly in a heavy skillet or electric frypan. *Serves 4.*

HOT HAM SALAD ROLLS

3 cups ground cooked ham
1 pound Cheddar cheese
12 frankfurter rolls
Butter or margarine softened

3 small dill pickles or 1 large
⅓ cup prepared mustard
⅓ cup mayonnaise

1. Cut a thin slice from the top of each roll and hollow out the rest of the roll. Spread both tops and hollowed shells with butter.
2. Grind the ham, cheese, and pickle together, and mix with mustard and mayonnaise.
3. Fill the rolls generously with this mixture and replace tops. Lay rolls on a baking sheet and heat 10 minutes in a 375° oven. Or chill and serve cold. *12 rolls.*

 # EGGS

Eggs often play a leading role in summer cookery, providing delightful main dishes for both luncheons and dinners. Stuffed eggs, which are well represented in this section, are also popular to accompany other dishes, especially for buffet meals.

ASPARAGUS-EGG CASSEROLE

5 hard-cooked eggs sliced
16-ounce can white asparagus tips
    cut in 2
4 tablespoons butter
4 tablespoons flour

2 cups cream, or rich milk combined with a little asparagus liquid
⅛ teaspoon grated nutmeg
Salt and paprika to taste
½ cup bread or corn-flake crumbs
2 tablespoons butter

1. Melt the butter in a saucepan and stir in the flour. Blend in the cream or milk and asparagus liquid, season to taste with salt, pepper, and nutmeg, and stir until smooth. Fold in the asparagus.
2. Arrange the sliced eggs in a shallow casserole and pour the asparagus sauce over. Or use a medium casserole and make alternate layers of eggs and sauce, repeating until the ingredients are used up.
3. Sprinkle with crumbs and dot with butter. Heat 10 minutes in a 350° oven, or broil slowly under medium heat. *Serves 6.*

Note: A similar effect can be secured by using cream of asparagus soup, slightly thinned with light cream, instead of making the asparagus sauce.

BAKED EGG CASSEROLE

6 hard-cooked eggs sliced
½ cup mayonnaise
½ cup catsup

1 teaspoon lemon juice
¼ cup milk
½ teaspoon salt

1. Arrange the sliced eggs in a very shallow casserole or pie plate, slightly overlapping them.
2. Mix mayonnaise, catsup, lemon juice, milk and salt until they are well blended and pour over the eggs.
3. Bake about 15 minutes in a 350° oven and serve at once over fresh hot buttered toast or fluffy hot rice. *Serves 4.*

BAKED EGGS IN ONION SAUCE

6 hard-cooked eggs
2 medium onions chopped
4 tablespoons butter or margarine
3 tablespoons flour
¾ teaspoon salt

⅛ teaspoon pepper
2 cups rich milk
½ cup bread or corn-flake crumbs
¼ cup grated Parmesan cheese

1. Cook onions in butter over very low heat, but do not let them brown at all.
2. When the onions are transparent, stir in the flour, salt, pepper, and milk, stirring until sauce is thick and smooth. Put the sauce in a double boiler, cover, and let it cook 45 minutes over simmering water.
3. Slice the eggs or cut them in half lengthwise and spread in a shallow casserole.
4. Pour the sauce gently over the eggs, top with the crumbs, and sprinkle with cheese. The casserole can then be baked 10 minutes in a 400° oven, or browned briefly under the broiler. *Serves 6.*

DEVILED EGGS

12 hard-cooked eggs
1 teaspoon dry mustard
½ teaspoon salt
¼ teaspoon fresh-ground pepper

2 tablespoons butter or
margarine
3½-ounce can deviled ham
3½-ounce can deviled chicken
½ cup mayonnaise

WHEN you cook eggs to be stuffed, it helps to have the yolks well centered in the whites. This can be accomplished by gently stirring the eggs until they are boiling hard so that they roll from side to side.
1. Cut the eggs in 2 lengthwise and remove the yolks to a small bowl.
2. Mash the yolks and blend in the mustard, salt, pepper, and butter.
3. Divide the mashed yolks into 2 bowls. Stir the deviled ham into one lot and the deviled chicken into the other.
4. Fill the whites with the mixtures and chill well. *Serves 12.*

DEVILED EGGS IN ASPIC

The Eggs

3 hard-cooked eggs
1 tablespoon mayonnaise
½ teaspoon Worcestershire sauce
½ teaspoon prepared mustard
¼ teaspoon onion salt
Dash cayenne

The Aspic

1 envelope plain gelatin
¼ cup cold water
1 teaspoon chicken stock base or
1 chicken bouillon cube
1⅓ cups chicken broth
¼ cup dry white wine
1 tablespoon tarragon vinegar
¼ teaspoon salt
6 pitted green olives cut in two

THESE are dressy looking and make a delicious luncheon or buffet dish.
1. Make the aspic first. Sprinkle the gelatin over the cold water and let stand 5 minutes. Add the chicken stock base to the chicken broth

and bring to a boil, stirring occasionally. Remove from the heat and stir in the soaked gelatin. Stir until dissolved and add wine and vinegar. Season to taste and chill until it begins to set.

2. Split the eggs lengthwise and carefully remove yolks to a small bowl.

3. Mash the yolks well or press them through a sieve. Blend in the mayonnaise, Worcestershire sauce, mustard, onion salt, and a bit of plain salt if needed. Mix well and stuff the whites with the yolks.

4. Pour about ½ inch of the aspic into the bottom of a small ring mold (not an individual one, however). Lay the stuffed egg halves at evenly spaced intervals in the aspic, stuffed side down. Put 2 half olives between each 2 eggs, cut side up. Spoon the remaining gelatin carefully over and around the eggs and chill until firm, at least 2 hours.

5. Unmold on a serving plate and garnish with sprigs of watercress and wedges of tomatoes. Serve with more mayonnaise. *6 servings.*

DEVILED EGGS SUPREME

I.
6 hard-cooked eggs
1 teaspoon grated onion
1 teaspoon mild prepared mustard
1 tablespoon soft butter or margarine
1 scant teaspoon minced parsley
Salt and pepper
Mayonnaise

II.
3 tablespoons mashed sardines
½ small tin deviled ham or 1 tablespoon minced cooked ham
3 tablespoons chopped shrimp
3 tablespoons finely chopped mushrooms sautéed lightly in butter

1. Cut the eggs in two lengwhise and remove the yolks to a small bowl. Mash them well and mix with the remaining ingredients in Part I, seasoning to taste, using just enough mayonnaise to make the yolks blend smoothly.

2. Mix into the mashed yolks any *one* of the ingredients in Part II.

3. Fill the whites with the mixture, rounding the tops and covering the white clear to the edge. Chill at least an hour. *6 servings.*

EGG–LUNCHEON-MEAT SALAD LUNCHEON MOLD

I. 1 envelope plain gelatin
    1 tablespoon sugar
    ⅛ teaspoon salt
    ¾ cup hot water
    3 tablespoons lemon juice
    ½ cup mayonnaise
    1¼ cups finely diced or
        chopped luncheon meat
    1 cup diced celery

II. 1 envelope plain gelatin
    1 tablespoon sugar
    Dash salt
    Dash pepper
    1½ cups hot tomato juice
    1 tablespoon lemon juice
    4 hard-cooked eggs coarsely
        chopped

THIS luncheon or buffet dish is as attractive as it is good.

1. Make Part I first. Mix the gelatin, sugar, and salt, and add the hot water. Stir over low heat until the gelatin is dissolved. Add the lemon juice and chill until it begins to set.

2. Stir in the mayonnaise, luncheon meat, and celery. Pour into a loaf pan rinsed out in cold water and chill until almost firm.

3. Make Part II when the first mixture is beginning to set. As before, mix the gelatin, sugar, salt and pepper, add the hot tomato juice, and stir over low heat until the gelatin and sugar are dissolved. Chill until it begins to set.

4. Stir in the chopped eggs and turn into the loaf pan, on top of the meat layer. Chill until firm.

5. Unmold on salad greens and serve with mayonnaise. *4–6 servings.*

EGGS À LA RUSSE

6 hard-cooked eggs cut in halves
    lengthwise
1 cup mayonnaise
3 tablespoons chili sauce

1 tablespoon chopped onion or
    shallots
1 tablespoon chopped chives
1 tablespoon chopped parsley
1 tablespoon chopped green olives

LAY the eggs cut side down on a flat serving dish. Mix the remaining ingredients well, or put them in a jar and shake them hard, and pour over the eggs. Chill thoroughly and garnish with small lettuce leaves. *Serves 4.*

EGGS CONTINENTAL

4 hard-cooked eggs sliced
¾ cup soft fine bread crumbs or
  corn-flake crumbs
¼ pound mushrooms sliced
3 slices bacon slivered and cooked
  crisp

1 cup dairy sour cream
2 tablespoons minced parsley or
  chives
Salt and paprika to taste
½ cup grated sharp Cheddar
  cheese

1. Spread the crumbs in an 8-inch pie plate or small shallow casserole and arrange the sliced eggs on top.
2. Sauté the mushrooms lightly in the bacon fat. Stir in the bacon, sour cream, parsley, and salt and paprika to taste. Spread over the eggs.
3. Sprinkle the top with the cheese and more paprika and bake in a moderate oven, 375°, 15–20 minutes, or until the sauce is bubbly and the cheese melted. *Serves 4.*

EGGS DELMONICO

4 hard-cooked eggs sliced
1½ cups cheese sauce
½ tablespoon minced pimiento

4 slices fresh hot toast
¼ cup grated Parmesan cheese

1. Make the cheese sauce with 3 tablespoons butter, 2 tablespoons flour, 1½ cups milk, ¼-⅓ cup grated sharp Cheddar cheese, and seasoning to taste, preferably including a dash of dry mustard.
2. Blend into the sauce the Cheddar and pimiento and sherry.
3. Lay the toast in a flat casserole or serving dish, cover with the eggs, then the sauce, then the Parmesan cheese, and bake 10 minutes in a 450° oven, or until the sauce is bubbly. *Serves 4.*

EGGS DIABLO

4 hard-cooked eggs	Salt and pepper
2 tablespoons deviled ham or tongue	1 envelope plain gelatin
	1 cup chicken broth
1 tablespoon melted butter	2 whole cloves
2 drops onion juice	½ cup white wine

1. Devil the eggs: Split them lengthwise, remove the yolks to a bowl, mash them with the deviled ham, butter, onion juice, and seasoning to taste.
2. Stuff the egg whites with the mashed yolks and press halves together as smoothly as possible. Chill.
3. Soften the gelatin in ¼ cup of the chicken broth. Bring the rest of the broth to a boil with the cloves and dissolve the gelatin in it. Cool and add wine and seasoning to taste. Fish out the cloves.
4. Place 1 tablespoon of the gelatin mixture in each of 4 custard cups and chill until set. Place an egg in each cup and pour the rest of the broth around the eggs. Chill until firm.
5. Unmold the eggs from the custard cups and serve on a bed of torn-up greens. Garnish with slices of tomato and serve with mayonnaise. *4 portions.*

EGGS FLORENTINE

8 poached eggs	2 tablespoons butter or margarine
1 package frozen chopped spinach	1 cup Mornay sauce (See Eggs Mornay)
Salt and pepper	
Dash nutmeg	Grated Parmesan cheese

1. Cook spinach over very low heat in heavy skillet, turning the frozen block frequently until the spinach is just thawed. Drain well, pressing out as much water as possible. No water is needed if the heat is kept very low, or at most 2–3 tablespoons.

22

2. Season the spinach to taste with salt and pepper and nutmeg and blend in the butter.

3. Spread the spinach in a shallow flat casserole and lay the poached eggs on top.

4. Spread the Mornay sauce over the eggs, sprinkle with the Parmesan cheese, and brown the cheese briefly under the broiler. *4 portions*.

EGGS MORNAY

The Eggs

6 hard-cooked eggs
1 tablespoon butter or margarine
1 tablespoon olive or salad oil
1 tablespoon minced onion
¼ pound mushrooms chopped
2 tablespoons tomato purée
1 teaspoon chopped parsley
¼ teaspoon salt
⅛ teaspoon fresh-ground pepper

Mornay Sauce

4 tablespoons butter or margarine
2 tablespoons flour
½ cup milk
½ cup light cream
½ teaspoon mustard
Dash cayenne pepper
Salt
2 tablespoons grated Swiss cheese
3 tablespoons grated Parmesan

1. Halve the eggs lengthwise. Remove the yolks to a bowl and mash them.

2. Melt the butter, stir in the oil, and lightly sauté the onion. Then add the mushrooms and cook 2–3 minutes. Blend in the tomato purée, parsley, salt and pepper. Stir in the egg yolks and blend vigorously.

3. Fill the egg whites with this yolk mixture and arrange them in a shallow casserole.

4. Make a cream sauce of 2 tablespoons of the butter, the flour, milk, cream, mustard, cayenne and salt to taste. Stir in the Swiss cheese and half of the Parmesan, and continue to stir until the cheese is melted and blended into the sauce. Swirl in the remaining 2 tablespoons of butter until barely blended.

5. Coat the stuffed eggs carefully with this Mornay sauce. Sprinkle with the remaining Parmesan cheese and bake 10–15 minutes in a hot oven, 425°. *Serves 3–4*.

EGGS ORIENTALE

8 hard-cooked eggs
1 tablespoon anchovy paste
2 tablespoons mayonnaise
6 ripe olives chopped
1 tablespoon lemon juice
2 tablespoons chopped walnuts or pecans
3 tablespoons melted butter or margarine

2 tablespoons flour
1½ cups milk or chicken broth
Salt and pepper
1 tablespoon Worcestershire sauce
1½ cups cooked and broken-up shrimp
½ pound sliced mushrooms lightly sautéed

1. Cut the eggs in half lengthwise, remove the yolks to a bowl, and mash.
2. Mix with the mashed yolks the anchovy paste, mayonnaise, olives, lemon juice, and chopped nuts. Refill the egg whites with this mixture and arrange them in a shallow casserole or serving dish.
3. Make a cream sauce of the melted butter, flour, and milk or chicken broth, seasoning to taste with salt and pepper and the Worcestershire sauce. When the sauce is thick and smooth stir in the shrimp—either broken-up large shrimp or tiny shrimp whole. Add the mushrooms and pour over the eggs.
4. These eggs can be served either hot or cold. If you serve them hot, bake the eggs in the cream sauce 20 minutes in a 375° oven. If cold, chill well. *Serves 6.*

If hot, serve with buttered spinach noodles and a tossed green salad. If cold, serve with a vegetable salad and hot rolls.

EGGS STUFFED WITH CRABMEAT

9 hard-cooked eggs
1½ cups flaked crabmeat (fresh, canned, or frozen)
1½ teaspoons dry mustard

1½ cups minced celery
3 tablespoons minced green pepper
1 cup mayonnaise

1. Cut the eggs in half lengthwise, remove the yolks, and mash them or put through a sieve. Mix the mustard with the yolks and season to taste.
2. Combine the crabmeat, celery, green pepper, mayonnaise, and the yolks. Stuff the egg whites with this mixture and chill well. Garnish with tomato wedges and parsley or watercress. *Serves 6, counting 3 halves per serving.*

SCRAMBLED EGGS WITH CRABMEAT

6 eggs beaten well
½ cup coarsely flaked crabmeat
  (fresh, canned, or frozen)
3 tablespoons butter or margarine

¼ teaspoon curry powder
⅛ teaspoon paprika
¼ cup light cream

1. Melt butter in a heavy skillet and stir in the curry powder, crabmeat, and paprika. Simmer just a moment, stirring.
2. Combine the eggs and cream and stir gently into the crabmeat, continuing to stir until the eggs are just set. Keep the heat very low. *Serves 4.*

SWISS SCRAMBLE

6 eggs
¼ cup light cream
3 tablespoons butter or margarine
  Salt and pepper to taste

1 cup shredded Swiss cheese
4½-ounce can deviled ham
  Fresh hot toast

1. Break the eggs into the top of a double boiler and stir into them the cream, butter, salt and pepper. Cook over hot water until the eggs begin to thicken, stirring occasionally.
2. As the eggs begin to thicken stir in the cheese and ham, continuing to cook until the eggs are done.
3. Serve on hot toast. *Serves 4.*

EGGS TETRAZZINI

6 hard-cooked eggs sliced
¼ pound spaghetti cooked
1 small onion chopped
2 tablespoons butter or margarine
3 tablespoons flour

1½ cups rich milk
½ teaspoon salt
¼ teaspoon pepper
Grated Parmesan cheese

1. Spread the cooked and well-drained spaghetti in a buttered shallow casserole or deep pie plate.
2. Sauté the onion lightly in the butter, until it is soft but not brown. Stir in the flour and slowly blend in the milk. Season to taste.
3. Stir a third of the sauce into the spaghetti and mix well; spread a little more sauce on top of the spaghetti.
4. Arrange the sliced eggs carefully on top of the spaghetti, overlapping them a little. Cover with the balance of the sauce, sprinkle generously with the cheese, and heat to bubbling under the broiler. *Serves 4.*

EGGS VINAIGRETTE

6 hard-cooked eggs
1 small can flat anchovy fillets
¼ cup wine vinegar
¼ teaspoon salt

⅛ teaspoon pepper
¾ cup olive oil
1 tablespoon capers
1 tablespoon chopped parsley

1. Halve the eggs lengthwise and cross 2 anchovy fillets over each half. Chill.
2. In a jar shake the vinegar, salt, pepper, and oil well. Add capers and chill thoroughly.
3. Pour the chilled sauce over the chilled eggs, sprinkle with parsley, and serve at once. *Serves 6.*

These eggs are especially good on a buffet table, served with cold sliced meat and a hearty green salad.

LUNCHEON EGGS

6 eggs well beaten
1 teaspoon dry mustard
1 cup heavy cream
¾ cup soft sharp Cheddar cheese

2 tablespoons butter
2 teaspoons fresh chives minced
1 teaspoon minced fresh chervil, or
⅓ teaspoon dried

1. Combine the mustard with the cream and pour half of it into a buttered shallow casserole. Crumble the cheese into it and add the butter in tiny dabs.
2. To the beaten eggs add the chives and chervil and pour carefully over the cream mixture in the casserole.
3. Bake in a moderate oven, 350°, 15–20 minutes, or until the eggs have formed a light crust.
4. Gently pour the remaining cream over and bake 10 minutes more, or until the eggs have a golden, puffy crust, but are not dry. *Serves 4–6.*

SMOKED-SALMON-CAVIAR-STUFFED EGGS

8 hard-cooked eggs
2 tablespoons lemon juice
1 teaspoon grated onion

Dash Tabasco
Smoked salmon
Black caviar

1. Halve the eggs lengthwise and discard the whites of two. Remove the yolks to a small bowl.
2. Combine the yolks with the lemon juice, grated onion, and Tabasco and season to taste.
3. Fill the whites with the yolk mixture. On top of each egg half stick a tiny cornucopia of smoked salmon and fill the cornucopia with caviar. *Serves 6.*

STUFFED-EGG LUNCHEON SALAD

6 hard-cooked eggs
1 teaspoon grated onion
1 tablespoon lemon juice
6 small sardines mashed

Salt and pepper
Mayonnaise
1 can condensed consommé
1 tablespoon plain gelatin

1. Halve the eggs lengthwise and remove the yolks to a small bowl.
2. Mash the yolks and blend in the onion, lemon juice, sardines, salt and pepper to taste, and enough mayonnaise to blend well. Fill the whites with this mixture and press together. Put each egg in a custard cup.
3. Add enough water to the consommé to make 1 pint. Soften the gelatin in a little of the consommé, heat the rest of it, and stir in the gelatin, continuing to stir until gelatin is dissolved.
4. Pour the consommé over the eggs and chill until firm. Unmold the eggs onto lettuce leaves and serve with tomato quarters. *6 servings.*

✤ MAIN COURSE DISHES

Unfortunately for the family cook, appetites are likely to be almost as demanding in hot weather as they are in cold, and a more or less substantial dish is usually in order for the main meal of the day, regardless of the weather.

Here are reasonably light main dishes in profusion, mostly ones that can be prepared early in the day or else require a minimum of time in their preparation. They include most meats, poultry, fish, and shellfish, both hot and cold. Another full section is devoted to main-course salads, which can be most welcome on a hot night.

BEEF

HAMBURGER RING

1½ pounds ground lean beef
2 eggs beaten
¾ cup milk
2 tablespoons minced onion

1 teaspoon Worcestershire sauce
1½ teaspoons salt
½ teaspoon paprika

1. Blend all these ingredients well and pack into a small greased ring mold.
2. Bake 1 hour in a 350° oven and turn out on a heated platter. *Serves 6.*

Fill the center of the ring with creamed mushrooms or succotash, and serve with a tossed green salad and sliced tomatoes.

SPECIAL HAMBURGERS

1½ pounds ground lean beef
  1 medium onion grated or minced
  1 tablespoon Worcestershire
    sauce

Salt and pepper
6 slices tomato
6 thin slices onion

1. Mix the beef with grated onion, Worcestershire sauce, pepper to taste, and about ¾ teaspoon salt. Handle lightly and form into 6 patties.
2. Put the patties under the broiler and brown on one side. Remove for a moment, turn, and put a slice of tomato, topped with a thin slice of onion, on the uncooked side.
3. Salt lightly and continue broiling until done the way you want them. *Serves 6.*

Serve with potato salad and corn on the cob, with sliced tomatoes and coleslaw. If you like, the hamburgers can be enclosed in hamburger rolls.

HAMBURGER SMITAINE

2 pounds ground round steak or
  chuck
2 tablespoons butter or margarine
  Salt and pepper to taste

½ cup minced scallions (green
  onions)
3 tablespoons tomato purée
1 cup dairy sour cream
  Paprika

1. Form the meat into 8 patties or 4 steaks and brown to taste in 1 tablespoon of the butter. Remove to a hot platter and salt and pepper to taste.
2. Lightly sauté the scallions in the remaining butter melted in the pan.
3. Blend the tomato purée and the sour cream into the scallions, cook just long enough to heat through, season with paprika, and pour over the steaks. *Serves 8.*

Serve with buttered hot noodles, green beans niçoise (see Index), and a tossed green salad.

JELLIED BEEF À LA MODE

4-pound piece of beef, eye of the round
2 tablespoons butter, margarine, or salad oil
⅓ cup cognac
3 cups dry white wine
1 veal knuckle if possible
2 teaspoons salt
½ teaspoon fresh-ground pepper
¾ teaspoon fresh chopped marjoram or ¼ teaspoon dried
¾ teaspoon fresh thyme chopped or ¼ teaspoon dried
1 small bay leaf
3 tablespoons chopped parsley
16 small white onions peeled
6 carrots quartered
2 teaspoons gelatin
3 tablespoons cold water

THIS is certainly not a "quickie" summer dish, but if it is made the day before it is needed it is a delicious item for a hot day's festive meal.

1. Brown the piece of beef on all sides in the fat in a Dutch oven or heavy skillet as you would a pot roast, and drain off any fat remaining.

2. Warm the cognac in a small pan, light it, and pour it flaming over the meat.

3. When the flames die down add the wine, veal knuckle, salt, pepper, marjoram, thyme, bay leaf, parsley, and enough water to almost cover the meat. Cover, bring to a slow boil, turn down the heat, and simmer for 1½–2 hours, or until the meat is almost tender.

4. Add the onions and carrots and continue cooking another half-hour, or until the meat is very tender.

5. Skim out the onions and carrots and arrange in the bottom of a mold. Strain the stock.

6. Slice the meat, not too thin, and arrange in layers over the vegetables.

7. Sprinkle the gelatin over the cold water and add it to 2½ cups of the hot gravy, stirring until the gelatin is dissolved. Pour over the meat and chill overnight. Unmold carefully on a serving platter and garnish with sprigs of parsley and tomato wedges. *Serves 8–10.*

Serve with baked sliced Idahos and buttered mixed vegetables (see Index).

BEEF, RICE, AND EGGPLANT CASSEROLE

1 pound ground lean beef
2 cups cooked rice
1 medium eggplant cut in 1-inch cubes, peeled and cooked in boiling water until just tender
5 tablespoons butter, margarine, or salad oil
½ cup minced onion

¼ cup chopped green pepper
1 tablespoon minced parsley
1 teaspoon salt
½ teaspoon pepper
½ cup bread or corn-flake crumbs
2 tablespoons grated Parmesan cheese

THIS is a flavorful casserole, and the rice makes it nearly a complete meal.
1. Drain and mash the eggplant.
2. Brown the beef in 3 tablespoons of the butter or oil. Add the onion and green pepper, and simmer until the vegetables are tender.
3. Mix together the eggplant, meat mixture, parsley, salt and pepper, and rice. Turn into a medium casserole.
4. Heat the remaining 2 tablespoons fat, stir in the crumbs, and spread on top of the casserole. Top with cheese and bake in a 375° oven 20–25 minutes, or until brown and bubbling. *Serves 4–5.*

Serve with green succotash (see Index), sliced tomatoes, and a tossed salad.

BRAISED BEEF GASCONY

3-4 pound eye-of-the-round beef
1 clove garlic
Salt and pepper
1 tablespoon bacon drippings
Pinch of nutmeg
¼ teaspoon cinnamon
3 cloves

Bouquet garni
1 tablespoon finely diced bacon
1 medium onion quartered
2 carrots cut in strips
¼ cup brandy
2 cups dry red wine
½ cup beef consommé

THIS delicious casserole needs to cook a long time, and is best done a day ahead, therefore, and just reheated slowly at serving time.
1. Rub the beef well with the cut clove of garlic and rub in salt and pepper.

2. Put the drippings in a large, heavy casserole, heat, and lay in the beef. Brown it lightly on all sides. Add the nutmeg, cinnamon, cloves, bouquet garni (2 sprigs parsley, sprig of basil, sprig of orégano, and small bay leaf tied in a little cheesecloth), bacon, onion, carrots, brandy, wine, and consommé. The beef should be almost covered at this point. Add a little more wine or consommé if not.
3. Cover the casserole with wax paper and tie it on. Set the cover on top of the paper. Bake in a 350° oven 1 hour, reduce the heat to 250°, and continue to bake 6 hours longer. Cool and chill until time to reheat next day. *Serves 10.*

Serve with potato salad and fresh asparagus with Hollandaise sauce.

BEEF IN HORSERADISH SAUCE

2 pounds round steak cut in 1½-inch cubes
2 tablespoons butter, margarine, or salad oil
1 large onion sliced thin
1 teaspoon curry powder (or to taste)
½ teaspoon ground ginger
1 teaspoon sugar

1 tablespoon Worcestershire sauce
½ teaspoon salt
¼ teaspoon fresh-ground pepper
1½ cups consommé
½ pint dairy sour cream
2 tablespoons prepared horse-radish
1 teaspoon minced parsley

THIS is an outstanding casserole, and not nearly as hot as it sounds.
1. Brown the meat in the fat and put in a heavy casserole, along with the onion, curry powder, ginger, sugar, Worcestershire sauce, salt, pepper, and consommé. Cover and bake in a slow oven, 300°, about 3 hours, or until very tender.
2. Stir in sour cream, horseradish, and parsley.
3. If you prefer the sauce a little thicker, knead a little flour and butter or margarine together and stir in until well blended and thickened. *Serves 6.*

Serve with fluffy hot rice and a cold vegetable salad (see Index). A tossed green salad is called for too, and hot buttered rolls or garlic bread.

JULIENNE BEEF IN SOUR CREAM

1 pound round steak cut in ¼-inch
   strips
1 small onion sliced
2 tablespoons butter, margarine,
   or salad oil

⅛ teaspoon ground ginger
1 teaspoon salt
Dash pepper
2 tablespoons flour
½ pint (1 cup) dairy sour cream

1. Sauté onion slices in butter, and stir in beef strips, ginger, and other seasonings. Stir frequently until meat is cooked and browned—10–15 minutes.
2. Stir the flour into the sour cream and blend into the skillet with the meat. Stir constantly until the sour cream is thoroughly heated. *Serves 4.*

Serve with Chinese noodles heated until crisp or fluffy hot rice, together with a mixed vegetable salad (see Index) and warm garlic bread.

SCOTTISH MEAT PIE

Pie Crust

¾ cup shortening
2½ cups flour
¾ teaspoon salt
⅓ cup cold water

Filling

¼ cup minced onion
2 tablespoons butter or margarine
1 pound lean ground beef
1 can condensed tomato or cream
   of mushroom soup
½ teaspoon salt
⅛ teaspoon pepper

1. Make the crust first. Cut ⅔ of the shortening into the combined flour and salt and blend until well mixed. Cut the balance of the fat into the flour coarsely.
2. Sprinkle the water, 1 teaspoon at a time, over the flour mixture and mix into dough. Continue this process until the dough is smooth.
3. Roll out a little more than half of the dough and line a deep pie plate.

4. To make the filling, cook the onion in the butter until soft. Add the meat and cook, stirring, until it is beginning to brown. Blend in the soup and seasoning and heat well. Turn into the pastry-lined pie plate.
5. Add the top crust, seal the edges, and prick well to let steam escape. Bake 40–45 minutes in a hot oven, 425°, or until golden. Serve hot or well chilled. *Serves 6.*

Serve with macaroni and cheese and buttered green beans if cold, and with potato salad, Italian green beans, and a tossed green salad if hot (see Index).

STUFFED GREEN PEPPERS

12 whole green peppers
2 pounds chopped lean beef
2 cups cooked rice
1 cup chopped green pepper
1 cup minced onions
½ cup catsup
2 tablespoons salt
¼ teaspoon fresh-ground black pepper
½ teaspoon dried thyme or 1 teaspoon fresh, chopped
3 eggs
2 cups tomato juice
2 cups water

1. Mix together well the beef, rice, chopped green pepper, onions, catsup, salt, pepper, thyme, and eggs.
2. Cut the stem ends off the green peppers, seed them, stuff them with the meat mixture, and arrange in a shallow casserole or baking pan.
3. Mix the tomato juice and water, pour over the peppers, and bake in a hot oven, 425°, until done—about 30 minutes, or until well browned. *Serves 12.*

Serve with well-beaten mashed potatoes, molded grapefruit-avocado salad (see Index), and a platter of sliced tomatoes garnished with French dressing blended with a mixture of fresh herbs chopped.

CHIPPED BEEF IN MUSHROOM SAUCE

¾ pound dried beef
¼ cup butter or margarine
2 cans condensed cream of mush-
    room soup
2 cups milk

1 teaspoon Worcestershire sauce
Freshly ground black pepper
2 egg yolks lightly beaten
½ cup slivered toasted blanched
    almonds

THIS recipe makes a real gourmet treat out of a prosaic meat.

1. Tear up the dried beef, cover it with hot water, and let it stand 10 minutes or so. Drain and discard water. Sauté the beef lightly in the butter for 2–3 minutes, stirring constantly.

2. Combine the soup and milk and stir until well blended. Add to the beef in the skillet. Season with the Worcestershire and a little pepper, but you are not likely to need salt. Simmer over very low heat for 4–5 minutes.

3. Beat the egg yolks lightly with a fork and stir in. Reheat a moment and serve over fresh buttered toast, fresh hot cornbread, or fluffy rice. *Serves 6.*

Serve with a vegetable salad mold (see Index) and a tossed salad to which thin tomato wedges and thin-sliced celery are added.

CHIPPED BEEF WITH CHEESE

¼ pound chipped beef
2 tablespoons minced onion
½ cup butter or margarine
3 tablespoons flour
1 cup milk

¼ pound mushrooms sliced and
    sautéed in butter or margarine
1 cup dairy sour cream
1 cup finely grated Cheddar
    cheese
2 tablespoons chopped parsley

1. Sauté the chipped beef and the onion in the butter until the onion begins to be transparent.

2. Blend in the flour and then the milk, and keep stirring until well blended and thick. Cook 5 minutes longer over low heat.

3. Stir in the sour cream and cheese, and stir until the cheese is melted and the sauce smooth. Blend in the cooked mushrooms.

4. Serve over hot buttered noodles, fluffy rice, hot toast, or toasted English muffins. Sprinkle with the parsley. *Serves 4.*

Serve with a bean salad (see Index) and baked cherry tomatoes with garlic (see Index).

QUICK SUPPER CASSEROLE

2 cups soft bread cubes
½ cup grated sharp Cheddar
2 tablespoons butter or margarine melted
1 cup cooked peas, green beans, or asparagus cuts
2 tablespoons minced onion
3 tablespoons butter or margarine

3 tablespoons flour
1½ cups milk
Salt and pepper
1 cup chopped cooked leftover meat, lucheon meat, or tuna fish
1 large tomato skinned and cut in ¼-inch slices

1. Mix together the bread cubes, cheese, and melted butter. Put half in a wide shallow casserole. Spread the vegetables on top.
2. Lightly sauté the onion in the 3 tablespoons butter, blend in the flour, add the milk slowly, and season to taste. Stir in the meat or tuna.
3. Pour the meat sauce into the casserole and cover the top with the sliced tomatoes. Top with the remaining cheese-crumb mixture and bake 25 minutes in a 350° oven. *Serves 4.*

Serve with a molded vegetable salad (see Index) and baked new potatoes (see Index).

HAM

BAKED HAM

THIS is a wonderful way to make a real old-fashioned country ham, not the modern "ready-to-eat" or "fully cooked" hams.

Skin the ham and lay it in a roaster or large pan. Lay 3 bay leaves and a dozen cloves on top. Spread with an 8-ounce jar of peach or apricot jam. Pour over it a bottle of dry red table wine, cover (with foil if no lid), and bake 25 minutes per pound in a 300° oven.

Forty-five minutes before the ham should be done, remove it from the liquid and lay it in a baking pan or large casserole. Spread the top thickly with brown sugar and drizzle ½ cup of honey over it. Return to the oven to brown for the remaining 45 minutes.

Serve with green succotash (see Index), quick scalloped potatoes (see Index), sliced tomatoes topped with French dressing mixed with fresh chopped herbs, and warm garlic bread.

BAKED HAM FOR A CROWD

WHEN you want to serve ham to a good-sized crowd, use a "tenderized" or "ready-to-eat" type. Slice it for serving before cooking it, or, far better, have your butcher slice it on his machine and put it back together again in its original shape, tying it around the sides at top and bottom.

Place the ham in the middle of a square of heavy-duty aluminum foil and bring the foil up the sides, but not across the top.

Spread the top thickly with peach or apricot jam and bake in a 350° oven 1 hour for a 6-pound ham, 1½ hours for a 10-pounder. *A 10-pound ham should serve about 15 people.*

Serve with a large casserole of bubbling macaroni and cheese and green beans niçoise (see Index). Warm French bread and a tossed green salad go well with this meal also.

GLAZES FOR BAKED HAM*

1. *Apricot Nectar.* 1 cup apricot nectar, 1 tablespoon sugar, and 1 teaspoon lemon juice. Cook until reduced by half. Spread on ham.
2. *Apricot.* Heat a jar of apricot jam; purée it in a blender, or rub it through a food mill. Spoon over the ham.
3. *Beer and Mustard.* Mix 1 cup sugar and 1 teaspoon dry mustard with enough beer to make a thick paste. Spread on ham.
4. *Brown Sugar and Sherry.* Mix 1 cup sifted brown sugar with ½ cup fine toasted bread crumbs and enough sherry to make a thick paste. Spread on ham.
5. *Honey.* Mix 1 cup warmed honey with 1 teaspoon dry mustard and ½ teaspoon ground cloves. Spread on ham.
6. *Brown-Sugar–Wine.* Mix ¾ cup brown sugar with ½ cup dry red wine or port and spread on ham.
7. *Pineapple-Sugar.* Blend ¾ cup crushed pineapple with ½ cup brown sugar and spread on ham.
8. *Bing Cherry Glaze and Sauce* To ¾ cup of cherry juice drained from a can of Bing cherries, blend in 2 tablespoons cornstarch, 2 tablespoons wine vinegar, and ¼ cup light corn syrup. Bring to a boil, simmer 4–5 minutes, and slowly stir in 2 teaspoons lemon juice.

Use ½ cup of this mixture to spread on the ham for a glaze. Add the cherries to the rest of the syrup, heat well, and pass as a sauce with ham.

* Glazes should be added to a baked ham only during the last half or three-quarters of an hour of the total cooking time.

PORT WINE SAUCE FOR HAM

½ cup port wine
1½ teaspoons minced shallots
    Sprig thyme
½ small bay leaf

Juice of 1 orange
Juice of ½ lemon
¼ teaspoon grated orange peel
1 cup consommé
1 tablespoon flour

1. Combine the port, shallots, thyme, and bay leaf, and simmer until the liquid is reduced by half.
2. Stir in the orange juice, lemon juice, and orange peel.
3. Mix a little of the consommé with the flour to make a paste. Add the rest of the consommé to the saucepan, heat, and stir in the flour paste to thicken the sauce slightly. Simmer 2–3 minutes before serving.

BAKED CANNED HAM WITH CHERRY SAUCE

1 canned ham
½ cup brown sugar firmly packed
½ cup honey

Sauce

1½ tablespoons cornstarch
¼ cup sugar
¼ teaspoon allspice
¼ teaspoon ground cloves
1-pound 4-ounce can sour red
    pitted cherries

1. Put the ham, fat side up, on a rack in a shallow baking pan.
2. Blend the brown sugar and honey and spread on the ham. Bake at 325° (1¼–2 hours for a 3–4½-pound ham, 2¼ hours for a 6¾-pound ham, and 2½–3 hours for a 10–12-pound ham).
3. To make the sauce, combine the cornstarch, sugar, allspice, and cloves in a saucepan. Stir in the juice drained from the cherries and cook until the sauce is thick and clear, stirring constantly.
4. Add the drained cherries, reheat, and pour over the ham on the serving platter.

Serve with corn on the cob, an avocado salad (see Index), and hot rolls.

BAKED HAM SLICE

Center cut of ready-to-serve ham
sliced 1½ inches thick
1 cup light brown sugar
2 teaspoons flour

1 teaspoon dry mustard
Dash fresh-ground pepper
Few drops vinegar
¼ cup water
Milk

1. Combine sugar, flour, mustard, and pepper, and spread half on the slice of ham. Sprinkle with vinegar and let stand 30 minutes. Place ham slice, treated side down, in a buttered shallow casserole, and spread the other side with the rest of the sugar mixture and a few drops of vinegar.
2. Bake the ham slice in a hot oven, 425°, 15 minutes.
3. Pour in the water, reduce heat to 375°, and bake 1 hour.
4. When the ham is done, remove it to a warmed platter, add a cup or so of milk to the sauce in the pan, and stir until smooth over low heat. Serve the sauce with the ham. *Serves 4–6.*

Serve with Italian green beans with water chestnuts, baked new potatoes, coleslaw (see Index), and buttered hot rolls.

BRANDIED HAM SLICES

2 slices ready-to-eat ham cut ½-
inch thick
2 tablespoons butter or margarine

⅓ cup honey
¼ teaspoon ground cloves
¼ cup brandy

THIS is a useful stand-by for a hot day, because it takes only a few minutes to prepare it.
1. Score the fat edges of the ham to prevent their curling.
2. Heat the butter in a large skillet, add the ham slices, and spread the top with half of the honey mixed with the cloves.
3. Brown the ham quickly, over high heat, turn, and spread the second sides with the rest of the honey-cloves mixture.
4. Warm the brandy in a small pan, light, and pour flaming over the ham. Serve as soon as the flames die down. *Serves 6.*

Serve with a mixed vegetable salad (see Index), potato puffs heated in a skillet, and a tossed green salad.

DANISH HAM WITH CHERRY HEERING

1 canned Danish ham, about 10   2 teaspoons dry mustard
   pounds   ¼ cup Cherry Heering
1 cup brown sugar

1. Remove the ham from the can, put it in a baking dish, and bake 30 minutes in a 350° oven.
2. Remove the ham from the oven and drain off any liquid that has accumulated.
3. Mix the sugar, mustard, and Cherry Heering and spread on the ham. Bake 30–45 minutes longer, basting often with the syrup in the pan. *Serves about 15.*

Serve with parsley-buttered little new potatoes, endive salad with beets (see Index), and party rolls, split, spread with garlic butter and grated Parmesan cheese, and lightly browned under the broiler.

DEVILED HAM ASPIC

1 can prepared tomato aspic   ¾ cup mayonnaise
   melted   4-ounce can deviled ham
1 envelope plain gelatin   1 teaspoon minced onion
½ cup cold water   ¼ cup minced sweet or dill pickle
½ teaspoon salt   1½ cups finely chopped cabbage
2 tablespoons lemon juice

1. Pour the melted aspic into a small ring mold and chill until almost set.
2. Sprinkle the gelatin on the cold water and dissolve over boiling water. Add the salt and lemon juice and cool.
3. When cool, stir in the mayonnaise, deviled ham, onion, pickle, and cabbage. Pour on top of the aspic and chill until firm. *Serves 4–5.*

Serve with tomato-egg mold, coleslaw (see Index), and crisped potato chips.

HAM AND CHICKEN CASSEROLE

1 cup diced cooked chicken
1 cup diced or julienned ham
2 cups fine noodles cooked
3-4-ounce can sliced mushrooms
4 tablespoons butter or margarine
1 tablespoon flour

1 cup evaporated milk
½ cup chicken broth
¼ teaspoon Tabasco sauce
2 tablespoons diced pimiento
1 teaspoon salt
¼ cup grated Parmesan cheese

1. Mix together the chicken, ham, noodles, and mushrooms and arrange in a shallow casserole.
2. Melt 3 tablespoons of the butter in a skillet, blend in the flour, and slowly stir in the evaporated milk and chicken broth. Stir over low heat until smooth and thickened. Add the Tabasco and pimiento, and season to taste.
3. Pour the sauce over the chicken-ham mixture in the casserole, top with cheese, dot with the remaining tablespoon of butter, and bake 20 minutes in a 375° oven. *Serves 4.*

Serve with a broccoli or asparagus casserole (see Index), a large tossed salad, and a macaroni salad (see Index).

HAWAIIAN TERIYAKIS

2-pound canned ham cut in 48
  one-inch cubes
1-pound-4½-ounce can pineapple
  chunks and syrup

½ teaspoon ground ginger
2 teaspoons sugar
½ teaspoon garlic salt
2 tablespoons soy sauce

1. Drain the pineapple but save the syrup. Combine the syrup with the ginger, sugar, garlic salt, and soy sauce. Into this marinade put the ham cubes and marinate them ½ hour.
2. Drain the ham cubes and thread them, alternately with the pineapple cubes, on skewers, using 3 of each to an 8-inch skewer.
3. Broil 4 inches from the heat, about 3–4 minutes on each side. *Makes 16 skewers or 8 servings.*

Serve with green succotash and zucchini with artichoke hearts (see Index), as well as a tossed green salad and warm garlic bread.

HAM AND CORN WITH NOODLES

1½ cups cubed canned or leftover
    cooked ham
12-ounce can whole-kernel corn or
    1 package cut corn cooked
3 tablespoons butter or
    margarine
1 large onion chopped

½ green pepper chopped
¼ cup flour
2½ cups milk
½-1 teaspoon curry powder
    Salt and pepper
3-ounce can chow mein noodles

1. Melt the butter in a skillet and cook the onion and green pepper about 5 minutes, or until onion begins to look transparent.
2. Stir in flour and slowly add milk, stirring until the sauce is smooth and thickened. Add the ham, corn, curry powder and salt and pepper to taste. Heat well.
3. Crisp the Chinese noodles in the oven and serve the ham-corn mixture over them. *Serves 4.*

Serve with a cucumber and pineapple mold and a Greek salad platter (see Index).

HAM JUBILEE

2½-pound slice of ham
    1-pound-4-ounce can black
      cherries, pitted
¼ teaspoon each ground cloves,
    curry powder, cinnamon, and
    dry mustard

1 tablespoon wine vinegar
1 cup currant jelly
½ cup orange juice
2 tablespoons grated orange rind

1. Arrange the ham in a shallow casserole a little larger than the ham.
2. Combine the juice drained from the cherries with the spices, vinegar, jelly, and orange juice. Bring to a boil in a saucepan.
3. Pour the hot mixture over the ham and bake 30 minutes in a 350° oven.
4. Add the cherries, mixed with the orange rind, to the casserole and bake another ½ hour. *Serves 6.*

Serve with a grapefruit ring mold (see Index) and a tossed green salad.

44

HAM RING WITH POTATO SALAD

2 cups minced or ground lean
  cooked ham
1 envelope plain gelatin
¼ cup cold water
1½ cups dairy sour cream

¼ teaspoon each salt and onion
  salt
¼ teaspoon celery salt
1 teaspoon prepared mustard
  Shredded lettuce
  Potato salad (See Index)

1. Soften the gelatin in cold water and dissolve over boiling water. Stir into the sour cream.
2. Add to the sour cream the ham and all the seasonings. Blend well and pour into an oiled ring mold and chill until firm.
3. Unmold the ring on a bed of shredded lettuce and fill the center with potato salad. Serve with mayonnaise. *Serves 6.*

Serve with green beans almondine and foil-roasted corn (see Index).

HAM AND VEGETABLE RING

3 cups ground cooked ham
1 stalk celery with leaves
1 medium onion peeled
½ green pepper, seeds removed
1 medium carrot

3 eggs
3 cups soft bread crumbs
¾ cup milk
  Salt and pepper

1. Use a medium blade to grind the ham. Using the same knife, grind the celery, onion, green pepper, and carrot.
2. Mix the eggs, crumbs (make fresh bread crumbs in your blender), and milk and stir into the ham mixture. Season to taste.
3. Turn into a well-greased medium ring mold and bake in a moderate oven, 350°, until firm in the center, about 45 minutes.
4. Turn out on a hot platter and fill the center with creamed eggs or creamed mushrooms. *Serves 6.*

Serve with buttered green peas and a large tossed salad to which tomato wedges have been added.

HAM MOUSSE

2 tablespoons gelatin
2 tablespoons Dubonnet or
    Madeira wine
1 teaspoon lemon juice
½ cup hot chicken broth
2 eggs separated

½ cup mayonnaise
5 dashes Tabasco sauce
1 cup diced ham
1 thin slice onion
½ cup heavy cream

THIS is an easy dish to make, since most of the work is done in a blender, and it is a delectable main course for a company meal on a hot night.

1. Put the gelatin, wine, lemon juice, and hot broth in the container of a blender and blend on high speed 40 seconds.

2. Add the yolks of the eggs, mayonnaise, Tabasco, ham, and onion to the blender and blend 20 seconds more on high speed.

3. Take out the center of the lid of the blender and pour in the cream with the motor on. Blend 30 seconds.

4. Beat the egg whites until they are stiff but not dry. Pour the mixture from the blender in gently and fold together until well mixed. Pour into a medium mold and chill until set. Serve with more mayonnaise. *Serves 6.*

Serve with an avocado salad (see Index) and macaroni and cheese.

LAMB

BONED LEG OF LAMB

A ROAST leg of lamb is an excellent choice for a fairly standard dinner in even the hottest weather. When the leg of lamb is *boned,* which your butcher can do easily, it offers no problems in carving.

Have the butcher bone and roll a 4-pound leg of lamb and send the bones along. Sprinkle the roast with thyme and insert slivers of garlic into slits cut with a sharp-pointed knife. Rub the surface of the lamb with salt and pepper.

Lay the bones in a roasting pan and arrange the lamb roll on top of them. Pour over 1 cup of consommé or water and roast in a 380° oven 20 minutes to the pound, or until a meat thermometer reads 180°—medium.

Remove the leg of lamb from the roasting pan after an hour, discard the bones, and pour the juices into a small saucepan. Cook them over quite high heat until the sauce thickens, continuing to roast the lamb meantime. Serve the sauce separately. *Serves 8.*

Serve with summer squash, coleslaw (see Index), a tossed green salad, and hot rolls.

SPIT-ROASTED SPRING LAMB

5-6-pound leg of spring lamb
   Salt and pepper to taste
½ cup melted butter or margarine

½ cup dry white wine
Fresh tarragon leaves (optional)

1. Fasten the leg of lamb securely on the spit and rub it well with salt and pepper.
2. Blend the butter, wine, and tarragon leaves, and use this mixture to baste the roast, beginning 1 hour after roasting begins, with heat set at medium (350°).
3. Spit-roast the leg of lamb on medium heat 2 hours and 40 minutes for rare and 3 hours for medium or well done. Let stand on the spit 10 minutes after it is done before carving. *Serves 10.*

Serve with macaroni and vegetable salad (see Index), parsley-buttered little new potatoes, and warm garlic bread.

SHASHLIK WITH BULGUR (Cracked Wheat)

2 pounds boneless leg of lamb cut
    in 1-inch cubes
½ cup French dressing
1 small bay leaf crumbled
4-8 large mushrooms caps

1 green pepper cut in squares
1-2 large tomatoes quartered
1 teaspoon Worcestershire
½ cup catsup

SHASHLIK is a Russian version of the Middle Eastern shish kebab, and is very similar to it.

1. Mix the French dressing and the bay leaf to make a marinade, mix in the cubed lamb, and let stand all day or overnight.

2. When you begin dinner preparations, drain the lamb (save the marinade), let dry a bit on paper towels, and thread on skewers, alternating the meat with halved or quartered mushroom caps and squares of green pepper. Put ¼ tomato at each end of each skewer. Brush the whole with the marinade before putting under the broiler (4 inches from the heat) or over charcoal on the grill.

3. Continue to broil, brushing occasionally with the marinade and turning the skewers occasionally. Allow about 15 minutes for broiling. The meat is done when it is crisp and brown on the outside.

4. Mix the Worcestershire sauce with the catsup and brush the meat with this sauce the last 2 or 3 times before it is done.

5. Make the bulgur (see Index) and serve the shashlik over it. Serves 8.

Serve with molded grapefruit-avocado salad (see Index), sliced tomatoes, and a tossed green salad.

SHISH KEBAB WITH RICE

2½ pounds lamb cut from leg or
    shoulder
Chopped parsley
Chopped onion
Thyme
Orégano
Dry white wine

Small fresh mushrooms
Bay leaves
4 tablespoons butter or
    margarine
1½ cups raw rice
Olive or salad oil

SHISH kebab is one of the most delightful ways to serve lamb, especially for a hot-weather meal.

1. In a medium casserole arrange a layer of chopped parsley to cover the bottom, cover the parsley with a thin layer of chopped onion, and sprinkle with chopped thyme and orégano.

2. Cut the lamb into 1- or 1½-inch cubes and arrange on top of the herbs in the casserole. Pour over dry white wine just to cover the lamb, cover, and refrigerate anywhere from 1 to 3 days, stirring each day.

3. Drain the lamb dry, saving the marinade, and arrange the cubes on skewers, alternating lamb with mushrooms. Put a small piece of bay leaf next to each lamb piece.

4. Strain the marinade and add the solid part to a skillet with the butter. Simmer until the onions are golden.

5. Stir in the dry rice and let it brown lightly 4–5 minutes, stirring almost constantly.

6. Add enough water to the liquid part of the marinade to make 3 cups, and add this to the rice. Let it boil up, turn heat to low, cover, and simmer gently 20–25 minutes, until rice it tender.

7. While rice is cooking, put the shish kebab under the broiler, brush with oil, and broil about 4 inches from the heat 15 minutes, turning to brown on all sides. *Serves 6.*

Serve with avocado mousse (see Index) and fluffy buttered hot rice.

POULTRY

QUICK CHICKEN CASSEROLE

2 packages frozen chicken à la
king
½ cup top milk or light cream
1 cup chicken broth
1 teaspoon Worcestershire sauce
Salt to taste

2 tablespoons sherry
½ package thin spaghetti cooked
Grated Parmesan cheese
Butter
Paprika

1. In the top of a double boiler put the chicken à la king, cream, broth, Worcestershire sauce, and salt to taste. Heat well and stir in sherry.
2. Drain the spaghetti and put ⅓ of it in a buttered 2-quart casserole. Cover with ⅓ of the chicken, and repeat twice.
3. Sprinkle the top generously with the cheese, dot with butter, and sprinkle with paprika. Put under the broiler until brown and bubbly. *Serves 6.*

Serve with fresh asparagus salad and endive salad with beets (see Index).

BOSTON CHICKEN

2 two-pound fryers cut up
3 tablespoons salad oil
½ cup tarragon vinegar
½ cup lemon juice
2 eggs slightly beaten
1 tablespoon water
2 cups bread or corn-flake crumbs
½ cup butter or margarine

½ cup chopped onion
Salt and pepper
¾ pound mushrooms sliced
10-ounce package frozen artichoke halves thawed
1 can cream of mushroom soup
1¼ cups light cream
¼ cup dry sherry

50

THIS casserole is a little fussy to put together, but it can be readied for the oven in the morning and is so good it is worth the trouble to make.
1. Combine the oil, vinegar, and lemon juice in a large bowl. Stir in the chicken, making sure each piece is moistened. Refrigerate, covered, for 2 hours.
2. Remove the chicken pieces from the marinade to paper towels to drain (save the marinade). With a fork beat the eggs with the water. Dip the chicken pieces in the egg and roll in 1½ cups of the crumbs.
3. Heat the ½ cup butter in a skillet and lightly brown the onions and mushrooms until they are golden.
4. Put 2 tablespoons of the marinade in the bottom of a large shallow casserole and arrange on it all the chicken pieces, the mushrooms and onions, and the artichokes. Salt and pepper the chicken to taste.
5. Combine the soup, cream, and sherry and pour on top of the chicken. Cover and bake about 45 minutes in a moderate oven, 350°.
6. Uncover the casserole, sprinkle with the remaining ½ cup of crumbs, and bake 15 minutes longer, uncovered. *Serves 6.*

Note: To make a real party dish of this recipe, use 3 whole chicken breasts (6 halves) instead of the cut-up fryers. The remaining ingredients are the same.

Serve with buttered green peas and salade niçoise (see Index).

QUICK CHICKEN BREASTS ALMONDINE

3 whole chicken breasts (6 halves)   ¼ cup blanched almonds chopped
1 can cream of mushroom soup   Salt and pepper

1. Lay the chicken breasts in a shallow casserole that will take them without overlapping. Salt and pepper lightly.
2. Heat the soup and pour over the chicken. Top with the almonds and bake about 1¼ hours in a moderate oven, 350°. *Serves 6.*

Serve with frozen potato puffs and an avocado salad (see Index).

CHICKEN BREASTS GRAND MARNIER

2 whole chicken breasts (4 halves)
2 tablespoons butter or
  margarine
1 teaspoon salt
½ teaspoon paprika
1½ cups chopped onion

⅓ cup evaporated milk
1 egg yolk
1 tablespoon lemon juice
1 tablespoon frozen orange juice
3 tablespoons Grand Marnier
  liqueur

1. Brown the chicken in sizzling butter, and sprinkle it with salt and paprika.
2. Spread half the onion in a shallow greased casserole, lay in the chicken, skin side up, and pour over the rest of the onion. Cover and bake 50–55 minutes in a 350° oven.
3. Combine the evaporated milk, egg yolk, lemon and orange juice, and Grand Marnier. Drizzle over the chicken and bake, uncovered, 15 minutes longer. *Serves 4.*

Serve with peas orégano and avocado salad (see Index), with a tossed green salad and warm garlic bread or buttered toasted rolls.

CHICKEN BREASTS ON NOODLES

3 whole chicken breasts split
¼ cup butter or margarine
½ pound medium noodles cooked
  Salt and pepper
1 pound mushrooms chopped
1 tablespoon chopped onion
1 tablespoon chopped parsley
½ cup fine bread or corn-flake
  crumbs

3 tablespoons butter or margarine
3 tablespoons flour
3 cups milk scalded
½ teaspoon salt
2 eggs yolks
½ cup cream whipped
½ cup grated Parmesan cheese

1. Mix a little of the ¼ cup of butter with the noodles and arrange them in a medium casserole.
2. Melt the rest of the ¼ cup of butter in a skillet and sauté the chicken breast halves about 25 minutes, or until they are tender and

golden brown. Lay them on top of the noodles. Season them with salt and pepper.

3. In the butter remaining in the skillet sauté the mushrooms and onion. Stir in the parsley and crumbs and season to taste. Spread mixture over the chicken breasts.

4. Make a cream sauce in the skillet of the 3 tablespoonsful butter, flour, milk, and salt. Blend in the egg yolks and whipped cream and stir until thick and smooth. Check seasoning and pour over the casserole.

5. Sprinkle with cheese and brown under the broiler.

If you prepare the casserole in the morning let it come to room temperature (1 hour) before cooking, and then bake it 30 minutes in a 300° oven before putting it under the broiler. *Serves 6.*

Serve with potato salad, lemon carrots (see Index), a plain tossed green salad, and warm garlic bread.

QUICK CHICKEN BREASTS IN SOUR CREAM

2 whole chicken breasts split
3-ounce can sliced mushrooms
   drained
    Salt and pepper

1 can condensed cream of mushroom soup
½ soup can dry sherry
1 cup dairy sour cream
   Paprika

1. Arrange the half breasts in a shallow casserole large enough to hold them without overlapping. Sprinkle the mushrooms over. Season to taste.

2. Blend well the soup, sherry, and sour cream. Heat and pour over the chicken. Dust with paprika, cover, and bake 1½ hours at 350°. Uncover the last 15 minutes. *Serves 4.*

Serve with fluffy hot rice and a mixed vegetable salad (see Index).

EASY CHICKEN CURRY (From Cans)

12-ounce can chicken cut in large
    pieces
1 can condensed cream of chicken
    soup
6-ounce can evaporated milk
½ cup chicken broth

½-1 teaspoon curry powder
9-ounce can pineapple chunks
    drained
½ cup chopped ripe olives
2 cans Chinese noodles

1. Combine and heat slowly the soup, evaporated milk, chicken broth, and curry powder to taste.
2. Still over low heat, stir in the pineapple, olives, and chicken.
3. Heat the noodles to crisp them and serve the curry over them. *Serves 4.*

The usual condiments to serve with curry include chutney, fresh coconut, chopped salted peanuts, preserved or candied ginger, poppadums (large thin wafers from India, for which toasted and buttered pilot crackers serve well), and Bombay duck, which is not duck at all but a dried fish from India, for which shredded dried codfish makes an acceptable substitute. A large green salad is needed to offset the hot curry.

SESAME FRIED CHICKEN

2 three-pound chickens quartered
4 tablespoons sesame seeds
    toasted
1¼ cups flour
½ teaspoon paprika

1½ teaspoons salt
    Fresh-ground black pepper
⅔ cup evaporated milk
½ cup butter or margarine
½ cup salad oil

1. Combine in a soup plate the toasted sesame seeds, flour, paprika, salt and pepper.
2. In another soup plate put the evaporated milk. Dip the chicken pieces in the milk and roll them in the flour mixture.
3. Heat the butter and oil in a large heavy skillet and brown the chicken pieces well on all sides, turning frequently. *Serves 6.*

Serve with corn on the cob and zucchini-tomato salad (see Index).

COLD CHICKEN PIE

3 cups diced cooked chicken
  Pastry for 9-inch pie
2 eggs beaten
½ cup dry white wine
½ cup heavy cream

½ cup cooked peas
4 hard-cooked eggs chopped
1 teaspoon salt
¼ teaspoon pepper

COLD meat pies, long a British and Scottish tradition, are not as generally served in this country as our hot summer weather would seem to call for.
1. Line a 9-inch pie plate with pastry.
2. Combine all the remaining ingredients, correct the seasoning, pour into the pie shell, cover with the top crust, seal the edges well, gash the top to allow the steam to escape, and bake 10 minutes in a 425° oven.
3. Reduce the heat to 350° and bake 30 minutes longer. Cool and chill. *Serves 4–6.*

Serve with bubbling macaroni and cheese or a baked rice casserole and a green pea salad (see Index).

CORN-CRISPED OVEN-FRIED CHICKEN

3-pound broiler-fryer, cut in
  pieces
1 cup corn-flake crumbs

1½ teaspoons salt
¼ teaspoon pepper
½ cup evaporated milk

1. Mix the crumbs, salt, and pepper.
2. Dip the chicken pieces in the milk and then roll in the crumbs. Lay the chicken pieces in a shallow baking pan lined with aluminum foil, and bake at 350° 1 hour or until tender. *Serves 4.*

Serve with Swiss cheese and potato salad, peas orégano (see Index), and a plain tossed green salad.

IMPERIAL CHICKEN

4-pound chicken cut for frying
2 cups fresh bread crumbs
¾ cup grated Parmesan cheese
¼ cup minced parsley
1 clove garlic minced or mashed

2 teaspoons salt
Pepper to taste
¼ pound butter or margarine,
melted

THIS is an easy and delicious dish, but it needs fresh soft bread crumbs, which can readily be made in your blender.
1. Mix the bread crumbs, cheese, parsley, garlic, salt and pepper.
2. Dip the chicken pieces in the melted butter and roll them well in the crumb mixture. Arrange in a large shallow casserole or baking pan, spaced so that the pieces do not touch.
3. Drizzle any leftover butter over the chicken and bake 1 hour in a 350° oven. *Serves 6.*

Serve with parsley-buttered little new potatoes and a tomato-egg mold, along with green salad with sour cream dressing (see Index).

BLENDER CHICKEN-ALMOND MOUSSE

2 envelopes plain gelatin
½ cup boiling water
¼ teaspoon pepper
1 thin slice onion
½ cup blanched slivered almonds

2 eggs
1 cup chicken broth
1 large cup cooked chicken (canned
will do)
1 cup heavy cream

1. Put the gelatin, boiling water, pepper, and onion in the container of the blender and blend on high speed 40 seconds.
2. Add to the container the almonds and eggs, cover, and blend 20 seconds.
3. Add the chicken stock and chicken, cover, and turn motor on high.

4. Remove the cover, or the little center piece of the cover, and pour in the cream, leaving the motor on high. Blend 30 seconds with the cream, pour into a mold rinsed out in cold water, and chill until firm. *Serves 6.*

Serve with an avocado, fig, and grapefruit salad mold (see Index) and party rolls split, spread with garlic butter and Parmesan cheese, and lightly toasted.

QUICK SUMMER CASSEROLE

1 cup cooked chicken or chunk-style tuna cut up	4 minced scallions (green onions) or 2 minced shallots
1 cup cooked ham diced small	½ cup light cream or evaporated milk
1½ cups cooked macaroni or spaghetti	1 tablespoon minced parsley
2 tablespoons butter or margarine	½ teaspoon salt
3-ounce can sliced mushrooms drained (save the liquid)	⅛ teaspoon pepper
	½ cup bread or corn-flake crumbs
	¼ cup grated sharp Cheddar cheese

1. Melt the butter in a saucepan and lightly sauté the mushrooms and scallions.
2. Stir in the chicken or tuna, ham, macaroni or spaghetti, cream, parsley, and salt and pepper to taste. Add some of the mushroom liquid if it seems a bit dry.
3. Pour the mixture into a medium casserole and top with the crumbs and cheese mixed.
4. Bake 15 minutes in a 325° oven and then put under the broiler a moment to brown the top. *Serves 4–5.*

Serve with a zucchini-cauliflower salad (see Index) and a platter of sliced tomatoes.

DE LUXE BROILED CHICKEN

3-pound fryer-broiler quartered
½ lemon
2 teaspoons salt
¼ teaspoon fresh-ground black
   pepper

Paprika
¼ cup melted butter or margarine
2 tablespoons sugar

1. Clean the chicken and wipe as dry as possible. Cut off wing tips. Rub entire surface of chicken with cut lemon, squeezing out a little juice as you rub.
2. Sprinkle the chicken pieces with salt, pepper, and paprika mixed. Coat with melted butter and then sprinkle with sugar.
3. Turn on the broiler and set the chicken pan under it but as far from the heat as the oven permits, to let the seasonings penetrate the chicken.
4. After 10 minutes move the pan up so that the surface of the chicken is 4 inches from the broiler heat and continue broiling. Baste occasionally with more melted butter, and turn several times. It should take about 35 minutes to broil a 3-pound chicken. *Serves 4.*

Serve with buttered green peas and Creole salad (see Index).

CHICKEN CONTINENTAL

3-pound chicken cut for frying
¼ cup lime juice (2 limes)
¼ cup lemon juice (1 lemon)
⅓ cup white wine
1 clove garlic mashed

1 teaspoon salt
¼ teaspoon dried thyme or
   ½ teaspoon dried tarragon
⅛ teaspoon pepper
¼ cup butter or margarine

1. Combine the lime and lemon juices, wine, garlic, salt, thyme or tarragon, and pepper. Lay the chicken pieces in a shallow casserole

and pour the mixture over them. Let stand at room temperature 30 minutes or in the refrigerator 1–2 hours.

2. Remove the chicken pieces from the marinade and arrange them in a shallow casserole or baking pan that will take them in a single layer, without overlapping. Dot them with the butter and bake 40 minutes to an hour in a 425° oven, or until tender. Baste with the marinade every 10 minutes. Pour the drippings over the chicken to serve it. *Serves 4–5.*

Serve with potato salad and avocado salad (see Index).

PRIZE BARBECUE CHICKEN

3-4-pound broiler-fryer chicken cut for frying	Salt to taste
3 tablespoons butter or margarine	1 cup catsup
2 tablespoons brown sugar	½ cup chopped celery
½ teaspoon mustard	1 medium onion minced
Dash cayenne	2 tablespoons vinegar
	¼ cup water

1. Sauté the chicken in the butter until golden brown.

2. Mix well the remaining ingredients and spread on the chicken. Cover the skillet, turn the heat very low, and simmer 30 minutes, turning the pieces occasionally.

3. Remove the cover of the skillet and bake the chicken in a moderate oven, 350°, about 35–40 minutes, basting frequently with the pan juices. *Serves 4–6.*

Serve with de luxe vegetable salad (see Index) and a platter of sliced ripe tomatoes, each slice topped with a dab of French dressing mixed with chopped fresh herbs.

CHINESE WALNUT CHICKEN

2 pounds solid chicken meat cut
  in small pieces (raw)
1 cup walnut halves
  Deep fat
2 teaspoons white wine

1 teaspoon salt
½ teaspoon cornstarch
½ cup butter or margarine
1 cup chicken stock
4 teaspoons cornstarch

THIS is an easy dish to prepare and has exceptional flavor.
1. Cover the walnuts with boiling water and a bit of salt. Let them stand 15 minutes, and then drain and dry them. Fry in deep fat until deep brown. Cool.
2. Mix the raw chicken with the wine, ½ teaspoon salt and the ½ teaspoon cornstarch combined.
    To this point the preparation can be done early in the day.
3. Heat the butter in a heavy skillet and sauté the chicken 1–2 minutes. Add the walnuts and cook 2–3 minutes longer.
4. In a saucepan combine the chicken stock, ½ teaspoon salt, and the 4 teaspoons cornstarch. Cook until thickened.
5. Pour the hot sauce over the chicken, cover, and simmer over low heat 20–30 minutes, or until the chicken is tender. *Serves 4.*

Serve with hot buttered rice, buttered green peas, and spinach salad (see Index).

CHINESE DUCK

5-pound duck
1 tablespoon soy sauce
1 teaspoon monosodium glutamate
  (MSG)
1 tablespoon minced leek or chives
  or scallions (green onions)
1 heaping tablespoon brown sugar
1 teaspoon cinnamon
  Pinch powdered cloves

1 teaspoon salt
⅛ teaspoon fresh-ground black
  pepper
2 teaspoons sherry
3 cloves garlic crushed
2 tablespoons soy sauce
2 tablespoons honey
1 tablespoon white wine, rum, or
  sherry

1. Scald the duck with boiling water 3–4 times and dry thoroughly, inside and out.
2. Mix the tablespoon soy sauce, MSG, leek, sugar, cinnamon, cloves, salt, pepper, sherry, and garlic and cook 2–3 minutes over a low flame. Spread it generously inside the duck and sew or skewer the cavity and the neck opening closed.
3. Mix the 2 tablespoons soy sauce with the honey and wine, and rub the outside of the duck.
4. Roast the duck in a 500° oven, uncovered, for 2–3 minutes. Then baste the duck with the honey mixture, cover it with a blanket of aluminum foil, and reduce the heat to 425°. Continue to bake 1 hour.
5. Uncover the duck and roast it 15 minutes longer, turning and basting it several times. *Serves 5–6.*

Serve with buttered noodles mixed with poppy seeds and slivered almonds, and a grapefruit-ginger salad (see Index).

BROILED DUCK QUARTERS

2 five-pound ducks, quartered	¼ cup olive oil
½ cup dry white wine	½ teaspoon ground ginger
¼ cup lemon juice	1 teaspoon salt

TRIM the excess fat from the ducks and place the pieces skin side down on the broiler rack. Broil at medium heat 15 minutes.

Mix the remaining ingredients and baste the duck pieces with the mixture. Turn the duck pieces over and broil 30 minutes longer, basting every 10 minutes. This broiling can also be done on a charcoal grill. *Serves 8.*

Serve with ginger ale fruit salad (see Index) and fresh asparagus.

ROTISSERIE DUCK

5-pound duck
½ cup olive or salad oil
½ cup sweet vermouth

Salt and pepper
Cloves
1 orange quartered, unpeeled

MIX the oil and vermouth and brush the duck well with it. Salt and pepper it, inside and out. Stick 1–2 cloves into each orange piece and place them in the cavity of the duck. Tie the bird securely on the spit and roast it about 1½ hours, basting frequently with the oil-vermouth mixture. *Serves 4–5.*

Serve with macaroni and vegetable salad and green beans almondine (see Index).

TURKEY-POTATO PUFF

1½ cups cooked diced turkey
3 cups fresh mashed potatoes
2 eggs separated
1 teaspoon grated onion
½ teaspoon dried thyme or 1½ teaspoons fresh, chopped

¼ teaspoon dried marjoram or ¾ teaspoon fresh, chopped
¾ teaspoon salt
½ cup turkey gravy
1 tablespoon melted butter

Now that turkey has become available around the year, it is an occasional summer treat, and leftover turkey becomes a problem. Here is a quick and easy way to use some of it.
1. Mix the fresh hot mashed potatoes (made with potato flakes if you want) with the yolks of the eggs, the onion, herbs, and salt. Fold in the egg whites, beaten until stiff but not dry.
2. Arrange half of the potatoes in a buttered 2-quart casserole. Cover with the turkey mixed with the gravy, and top with the rest of the potatoes.
3. Drizzle the butter over the top and bake 35–40 minutes in a slow oven, 325°, or until well browned. *Serves 6.*

Serve with a broccoli or asparagus casserole and a summer garden salad (see Index).

62

VEAL

EXOTIC VEAL

1½ pounds boneless veal cut in 1-
   inch cubes
2 teaspoons Kitchen Bouquet
2 tablespoons butter, margarine,
   or salad oil
¾ cup chopped onions
¾ cup sliced mushrooms
1 cup water, white wine, or
   mixture of both
2 tablespoons light brown sugar
¼ cup vinegar

½ teaspoon ground ginger
1 teaspoon dry mustard
1 teaspoon salt
¼ teaspoon fresh-ground black
   pepper
1-2 tablespoons cornstarch
2 tablespoons water
1 tablespoon dry red wine
1½ cups flaked coconut (optional)
5-ounce can water chestnuts
   sliced

THIS is an exceptionally delicious dish, and is a good choice for a buffet dinner or any company dinner.

1. Brush the veal cubes with the Kitchen Bouquet and brown them in sizzling butter, margarine, or oil in a large skillet.

2. Add the onions and mushrooms and cook until the onions begin to color.

3. Add the water or wine, sugar, vinegar, spices, salt, and pepper. Simmer, uncovered, over low heat, or until meat is tender.

4. Mix the cornstarch with the 2 tablespoons water and stir in, continuing to stir until the liquid is smooth and slightly thickened.

5. Stir in the red wine, coconut, and water chestnuts, bring just to a boil, and serve. *Serves 6.*

Serve with lots of hot fluffy rice to absorb the wonderful sauce, a molded salad (see Index) surrounded with torn-up salad greens tossed with French dressing, and hot buttered rolls.

ALSATIAN VEAL ROLLS

4 thin veal scallops
4 thin slices ham
4-6 ounces mushrooms chopped and
   lightly sautéed in butter or
   margarine

1 tablespoon butter or margarine
White wine
Salt and pepper

1. Pound the scallops very thin and lay a slice of ham on each slice of veal.
2. Sauté the mushrooms until the moisture has all evaporated and then spread them over the ham. Roll up the meat and fasten with skewers or twine.
3. Heat the butter in a heavy skillet and brown the veal on all sides. Salt and pepper lightly, add a little wine, cover, and simmer over very low heat about 1 hour, adding a little wine from time to time as needed. *Serves 4.*

Serve with baked sliced potatoes in foil, cucumbers in sour cream, and coleslaw (see Index).

COLD VEAL WITH TUNA SAUCE

3 pounds boneless veal rolled and
   tied
2 cloves
1 large onion
2 small bay leaves
2 carrots
2 stalks celery
6 sprigs parsley

2 teaspoons salt
½ teaspoon pepper
2 seven-and-three-quarter-ounce
   cans tuna
1 small can anchovy fillets
1 cup olive or salad oil
3 tablespoons lemon juice
1 tablespoon chopped capers

This Italian dish is almost a classic hot-weather dish, and should be prepared a day ahead, to allow it to marinate at least 12 hours.
1. Stick the cloves into the onion and put in a large saucepan with the veal roll, bay leaves, carrots (whole or cut in chunks), celery,

64

parsley, salt and pepper. Add water just to cover and cook slowly until the veal is tender, about 2 hours. Drain and cool.

2. Force the tuna fish and anchovies through a coarse sieve or purée them in a blender. Gradually beat in the oil and lemon juice until the sauce is creamy and smooth. Stir in the capers.

3. When the veal is cool, slice it very thin and pile up the slices in a large glass or crockery bowl. Pour the sauce over the meat, cover, and chill at least 12 hours in the refrigerator. Unmold on a serving platter. *Serves 6–8.*

Serve with a platter of sliced tomatoes, each slice garnished with a little French dressing mixed with fresh herbs, a large tossed green salad with a sliced avocado mixed in it, and hot garlic bread.

VEAL BIRDS WITH PINE-NUT STUFFING

6 slices veal from the leg	Salt and pepper
1 cup chopped parsley	½ cup pine nuts
½ cup chopped cooked ham	3 tablespoons salad oil
¼ cup raisins	½ cup Marsala or Madeira wine
¼ cup grated Parmesan or Romano cheese	

1. Pound the veal very thin and cut in pieces for rolls (about 2½ by 5 inches).

2. Combine the parsley, ham, raisins, cheese, salt and pepper to taste, and pine nuts to make the stuffing. Mix well and divide among the veal pieces. Roll them up and skewer or tie them securely.

3. Heat the oil in a heavy skillet and brown the rolls on all sides. When all are brown pour in the wine, cover the skillet, and simmer over very low heat about 25 minutes, or until the meat is fork tender. Remove the skewers or strings before serving. *Serves 8–10.*

Serve with buttered green peas, riced potatoes, and a molded vegetable salad (see Index).

VEAL CASSEROLE WITH BLACK GRAPES

1½ pounds boneless veal cut in
   1½-inch cubes
Flour
Salt and pepper
3 tablespoons butter or
   margarine

2 cups dry white wine
1 small bay leaf
Dash cayenne pepper
½ pound mushrooms quartered
½ pound black grapes peeled and
   seeded

1. Dust the veal cubes lightly, on all sides, with the flour, salt, and pepper, and brown in hot butter. Transfer to a medium casserole.
2. Add the wine, bay leaf, and cayenne to the skillet in which the veal was browned. Cook the mixture ten minutes, stirring to absorb all the brown particles, and pour over the veal.
3. Add the mushrooms and grapes to the casserole, cover, and bake 1 hour in a 350° oven, or until the veal is tender. *Serves 4.*

Serve with buttered noodles to which poppy seeds and slivered almonds have been added, a mixed vegetable dish (see Index), and a large tossed green salad to which are added sliced tomatoes and thin-sliced celery.

VEAL CASSEROLE WITH SOUR CREAM

2 pounds veal cut in 1-inch cubes
¼ cup flour
1½ teaspoon salt
¼ teaspoon pepper
2 tablespoons salad oil
2 medium onions sliced
1 package frozen cut corn
1 package frozen green peas

1 cup chicken broth
½ cup green pepper sliced very
   thin
¼ cup thin-sliced scallions (green
   onions)
¼ cup celery sliced thin diagonally
½ cup dairy sour cream

1. Put the flour, salt, and pepper in a paper bag and shake the veal pieces in it, a few at a time.

2. Heat the oil to sizzling and brown the veal pieces well on all sides. Transfer to a medium casserole, and add the onions, corn and peas broken up, and chicken broth. Cover and bake 45 minutes at 325°.
3. Stir in the green pepper, scallions, and celery, cover again, and bake 20 minutes longer.
4. When ready to serve, stir in the sour cream, correct seasoning, and reheat a moment on top of the stove, but do not let boil. *Serves 6.*

Serve with fluffy hot rice and a blender avocado ring mold salad (see Index).

VEAL CHOPS POITOU

4 veal chops cut 1-inch thick
2 tablespoons butter or margarine
3 shallots minced or 1 tablespoon
  minced onion
2 tablespoons diced cooked ham or
  diced bacon

Salt and pepper
½ cup veal or chicken stock
½ cup dry white wine
2 egg yolks lightly beaten
Few drops wine vinegar
1 teaspoon chopped parsley

1. Heat the butter in a heavy skillet and lightly brown the shallots and ham or bacon.
2. Season the chops and add them to the skillet, browning them slowly on both sides until they are done. Remove them to a heated serving platter.
3. Discard part of the fat in which the chops were cooked and add the stock and wine to the skillet. Turn up the heat and boil the liquid until it is reduced about one-fourth.
4. Mix a little of the hot liquid with the egg yolks, pour into the rest of the liquid, and stir constantly until the sauce is smooth and thickened.
5. Add the vinegar and parsley when ready to serve, stir in well, and pour the sauce over the chops. *Serves 4.*

Serve with frozen potato puffs and peas orégano (see Index).

SAVORY VEAL

4 pounds veal cut in 2-inch cubes
½ cup flour
2 teaspoons salt
½ teaspoon fresh-ground pepper
¼-½ cup salad oil
2 large onions chopped
4 medium carrots diced
4 stalks celery cut in ¼-inch slices
  diagonally
2 cups chicken broth

½ cup dry white wine
4 medium tomatoes skinned and
  chopped or 1 can Italian
  tomatoes
1 large clove garlic mashed
1 bouquet garni
2 tablespoons chopped parsley
2 teaspoons grated lemon rind
2 tablespoons lemon juice

1. Put the flour, salt and pepper in a paper bag and shake the veal pieces in it, a few at a time.
2. Heat the oil to sizzling in a large heavy skillet and brown the veal cubes on all sides. Do not crowd the skillet or the veal will not brown. Transfer to a large casserole as they finish browning.
3. In the fat remaining in the skillet lightly sauté the onions, carrots, and celery, stirring often.
4. Add to the skillet the chicken broth, wine, tomatoes, garlic, and bouqet garni (2 sprigs parsley, 1 sprig orégano, 1 leaf sweet basil, and 1 small bay leaf tied in a bit of cheesecloth). Bring to a boil and simmer 3–4 minutes. Pour over the casserole, cover, and bake 1¾ hours at 300°.
5. Check the seasoning about halfway through the cooking. Just before serving stir in the parsley, lemon rind, and lemon juice. *Serves 8–10.*

Serve with a large mixed vegetable dish and cucumbers with sour cream (see Index).

COLD VEAL AND HAM PIE

1½ recipes pastry
2 pounds leg of veal sliced very thin
¼ cup minced onion
¼ cup minced celery
¼ cup chopped green pepper
1 teaspoon chopped parsley
1½ pounds tenderized uncooked ham sliced thin

Salt and pepper
3 thin strips salt pork
1 tablespoon Worcestershire sauce
½ cup dry sherry
2 envelopes plain gelatin
2 cups consommé or chicken broth

1. Roll out the pastry ⅛ inch thick and line a 3-quart casserole with about ⅔ of it.
2. Unless the veal is cut very thin indeed, flatten it further between sheets of wax paper with a wooden mallet or the flat side of a cleaver.
3. Mix together the onion, celery, green pepper, and parsley.
4. Build up the casserole with alternating layers of veal, ham, and mixed vegetables, seasoning each layer lightly. Make a layer of the salt pork slices in the middle of the casserole.
5. Mix the Worcestershire sauce and sherry and pour over the casserole.
6. Soak the gelatin in ½ cup of the stock, combine with the rest of the stock, and heat until the gelatin is dissolved. Pour half of this liquid over the pie.
7. Roll out a top crust, cut a hole the size of a silver dollar in the center, and lay over the pie, sealing the edges well. Replace the cut-out piece loosely and bake the pie in a 350° oven 1½ hours. If it gets too brown, lay a piece of brown paper over it.
8. Every 30 minutes take the pie out of the oven, remove the center circle, and pour in more stock with a funnel. Cool and chill well. Serve either in medium wedges or in ½-inch slices. *Serves 12–15.*

Serve with a bubbling hot casserole, such as macaroni and cheese or spoon bread and Italian green beans with water chestnuts (see Index). A tossed green salad or a plate of chilled sliced tomatoes goes well too.

VEAL PARTY CASSEROLE

5 pounds boneless veal cut in 1½-inch cubes
⅓ cup salad oil
2 onions chopped or sliced thin
1 pound-4-ounce can Italian-style tomatoes
1 can tomato purée
1 small can tomato sauce
1½ cups chicken broth
½ cup dry sherry
1 cup dry white or rosé wine
1½ teaspoons salt
1 teaspoon Tabasco sauce
2 small bay leaves
3 teaspoons chopped fresh thyme or orégano or 1 teaspoon each dried
1 cup sliced celery
Paste of ⅓ cup flour and ½ cup water
½ pound mushrooms sliced or 2 four-ounce cans
2 one-pound cans tiny white onions drained
1 package frozen green peas thawed
1 package frozen cut green beans thawed

1. Brown the veal in sizzling oil, a few pieces at a time. Transfer to a large casserole as they are browned, or to 2 medium casseroles.
2. In the fat remaining in the skillet sauté the onions lightly. Stir in the tomatoes, tomato purée, tomato sauce, chicken broth, sherry, white or rosé wine, salt to taste, Tabasco, herbs, bay leaves, and celery. Bring to a boil, reduce the heat, and simmer about 5 minutes.
3. Stir in the flour-and-water paste, stirring constantly until the sauce is thick and smooth. Pour over the veal in the casserole or casseroles.
4. Cover the casserole and bake 1¼ hours in a 325° oven. At this point stir in the mushrooms and onions, cover again, and bake 10 minutes longer.
5. Stir in the peas and beans and continue to bake 10 minutes longer, uncovered. *Serves 12–14.*

Serve with a mixed vegetable casserole, such as Tian (see Index) and a large tossed green salad.

VEAL AND HAM SCALOPPINE

3 pounds veal cutlet sliced very thin
and cut into small squares
6 tablespoons butter or margarine
2 cups chopped onion
Flour
2 teaspoons salt
1 teaspoon garlic powder (or
2 cloves garlic mashed)

1½ teaspoons fresh marjoram
chopped or ½ teaspoon dried
½ teaspoon dried savory
3 cups cooked ham julienned
¼ pound butter or margarine
1 pound mushrooms sliced
4 cups diary sour cream

1. Sauté the onion lightly in the 6 tablespoons butter in a large skillet and transfer to a large saucepan or kettle.

2. In the fat remaining in the skillet lightly brown the veal pieces which have been lightly dusted with flour. Do not crowd the pieces in the pan. As the veal is browned add it to the onions in the saucepan. Stir in the salt, garlic or garlic powder, marjoram, savory, and ham and blend well.

3. Add the ¼ pound butter to the skillet and sauté the mushrooms lightly. Stir them into the meat, scraping the skillet to get all the brown particles.

4. Heat the meat mixture and stir in the sour cream, stirring constantly until smooth and well blended. Do not let it boil or it will curdle. Correct seasoning before serving. *Serves 10–12–15.*

Serve with Swedish bean salad (see Index) and scooped-out tomatoes stuffed with potato salad.

QUICK VEAL SCALLOPS WITH CREAM

2 pounds veal cutlet sliced very thin	4 tablespoons warmed cognac
Salt and pepper	1 cup heavy cream
6 tablespoons butter or margarine	

1. Pound the scallops very thin between sheets of wax paper and season them.
2. Heat the butter to sizzling in a heavy skillet and sauté the scallops quickly, not more than 3 minutes on each side.
3. Light the warmed cognac and pour over the scallops. When it burns out remove the scallops to a heated platter.
4. Pour the cream into the skillet, stir it well to get up all the brown bits, and pour over the veal. Serve at once. *Serves 6.*
Note: A nice variation of this recipe is to add to the skillet, instead of the cream, ⅔ cup dry white wine and boil it vigorously until it is reduced one-half. Swirl in 1 tablespoon chopped fresh tarragon and 2 tablespoons butter or margarine, and pour over the scallops.

Serve with buttered noodles, lemon carrots and coleslaw (see Index).

FISH AND SHELLFISH

BAKED FISH

Most medium and large fish are good for baking, and the method is the same for bluefish, mackerel, snapper, etc.

Split the fish but do not separate the halves if possible. Remove the backbone or have the fish prepared at the market. Salt and pepper the fish inside and out and score 3 or 4 times on each side to prevent shrinking.

Make a stuffing out of bread crumbs, crushed garlic, chopped chervil and parsley, salt and pepper, and just enough milk to hold it together. The quantities will depend upon the size of the fish, and the stuffing should be loose rather than compacted in the fish. Stuff the fish and either sew or skewer it closed.

Put a good-sized piece of butter in a baking pan about the size of the fish, melt it, and lay the fish in the melted butter. Cover it completely with thinly sliced onions. Add a 50–50 mixture of dry white wine and court bouillon (*see below*) until the fish is half covered. Cook uncovered in a 350° oven until the fish is fork tender. A 3-pound fish will take about 45 minutes, a 6-pound one an hour. Baste frequently. Sprinkle with chopped parsley before serving.

A court bouillon is made by boiling up and simmering briefly the trimmings of the fish, a little chopped celery, parsley, and thyme, ½ bay leaf, ½ cup dry white wine to a quart of water, a small onion, several whole peppercorns, pounded to bruise them, and salt. Strain through a double thickness of cheesecloth.

Fluffy mashed potatoes go well with baked fish. Serve also quick vegetable casserole (see Index) and a tossed green salad.

QUICK BAKED FILLETS OF FISH

THIS is the simplest possible way of providing a delicious hot fish dish. Put fine bread or corn-flake crumbs in a soup plate and milk or evaporated milk in another. Dip the fillets, cut into individual portions, first into the milk and then into the crumbs. Lay them on a greased cookie sheet, salt and pepper the fish lightly, and drizzle about 1 teaspoon salad oil over each piece. Bake 10 minutes in a hot oven (450°–475°) for thinnish fillets, like fillet of sole, and a little longer for thicker. Plan 1 fillet per person.

Serve with frozen French-fried potatoes and endive salad with beets (see Index).

DEVILED FISH STICKS

1 package frozen fish sticks	½ teaspoon lemon juice
2 tablespoons soft butter or margarine	Dash Tabasco
	1 tablespoon finely minced onion
⅛ teaspoon dry mustard	2 tablespoons minced parsley
¾ teaspoon Worcestershire sauce	

FISH sticks are a convenient item to have on hand in the freezer, but they can do with quite a bit of flavoring. This simple recipe turns them into a real treat.

Melt the butter partially and stir in the remaining ingredients. Don't worry if they don't blend into a perfectly smooth sauce. Lay the frozen fish sticks in a close row in a pie plate or on a cookie sheet and spread with the mixture. Broil 5–6 minutes about 4 inches from the heat, or until sizzling. They do not need to be turned. *Serves 2–3.*

Serve with buttered Italian green beans and summer garden salad (see Index).

HALIBUT FLORENTINE

PUT a slice of halibut about 1 inch thick in a shallow greased casserole. Sprinkle it with salt and pepper, white wine or sherry, and melted butter. Bake it 15 minutes in a moderate oven, 350°.

While the halibut is baking make a rich cream sauce, using 3 tablespoons butter or margarine, 2 tablespoons flour, and one cup top milk or evaporated milk. Stir in ½ package frozen chopped spinach just thawed. Pour over the halibut, sprinkle with grated Parmesan cheese and paprika, and bake another 10 minutes. *Serves 4.*

Serve with anchovy potatoes, salade niçoise (see Index), and a green salad.

BROILED HALIBUT

FOR 4 portions of halibut cut 1 inch thick, melt 6 tablespoons butter or margarine in a shallow casserole and stir in 1 cup dry vermouth. Lay in the fish pieces, stir them around and turn them over to make sure that they are well coated with the sauce. Salt and pepper the fish lightly and put under a preheated broiler, about 6 inches from the heat, and baste frequently with the butter-vermouth mixture. It should take about 20 minutes to cook, 10 minutes on each side. When the fish is just about done, remove the casserole from the broiler and sprinkle the fish lightly with fine bread crumbs and grated Parmesan cheese mixed 50–50. Return to the broiler and broil a minute or two more. *Serves 4.*

Serve with cucumber and grapefruit mold (see Index) and warm garlic bread.

DEVILED HALIBUT

2 halibut steaks 1 inch thick
¼ cup chopped green pepper
¼ cup minced onion
1 tablespoon prepared mustard
1 teaspoon Worcestershire sauce
⅛ teaspoon Tabasco sauce
3½ tablespoons lemon juice

½ cup butter melted
2 cups fine bread or corn-flake crumbs
2 tablespoons grated Parmesan cheese
Salt and pepper

1. Mix in a bowl the green pepper, onion, mustard, Worcestershire sauce, Tabasco, lemon juice, butter, and crumbs.
2. Season the top of the steaks and spread with half the crumb mixture. Lay in a shallow greased casserole, crumbed side down.
3. Season the second side and spread with the remaining crumb mixture.
4. Bake the casserole 25–30 minutes, or until the fish flakes easily with a fork, in a 325° oven.
5. Sprinkle the cheese over the top of the steaks and put under the broiler 3–4 minutes to brown. *Serves 4.*

Serve with quick scalloped potatoes and cucumber and grapefruit mold (see Index).

BLENDER SALMON MOUSSE

1-pound can salmon drained and
  broken up
1 envelope plain gelatin
½ cup boiling water
2 tablespoons lemon juice
1 small onion diced

½ cup mayonnaise
¼ teaspoon paprika
1 teaspoon dried dillweed or
  1 tablespoon fresh dill minced
1 cup heavy cream

1. Put into the container of the blender the gelatin, boiling water, and lemon juice. Cover and blend on high speed 40 seconds.
2. Turn off and add to the blender the mayonnaise, paprika, dill, and salmon. Cover and turn on the motor to high speed.
3. Remove the center of the lid, pour in the cream, and blend 30 seconds more. Pour into a small mold and chill until firm. Unmold and serve with mayonnaise. *Serves 6.*

Serve with baked sliced potatoes in foil, and ginger ale fruit salad (see Index).

SALMON RING WITH PEAS

16-ounce can salmon drained,
  picked over, and flaked rather
  fine
2 eggs slightly beaten
1 can cream of mushroom soup
¾ cup cracker crumbs
¼ cup chopped green pepper

1 tablespoon minced parsley
1 tablespoon lemon juice
1 teaspoon grated onion
Pepper
Celery salt
1 package frozen green peas

1. Gently combine the eggs, ½ cup of the soup, crumbs, green pepper, parsley, lemon juice, onion, a dash of pepper, and a good pinch of celery salt. Stir in the salmon and spoon into a well-buttered ring mold.
2. Bake the mold 40–45 minutes in a moderate oven, 350°, and unmold on a hot platter.

3. Cook the peas in ½ cup boiling water, letting them simmer 1–2 minutes after the water comes to a boil again. Drain and mix gently with the rest of the cream of mushroom soup, well heated but not boiled. The consistency will be improved if you dilute the soup a bit with a little light cream.

4. Pour the creamed peas into the center of the salmon ring and over the ring. *Serves 3–4.*

Serve with fluffy hot rice and cold cooked broccoli mixed with French dressing and a little mayonnaise.

SALMON STEAKS BRAISED IN WHITE WINE

2 salmon steaks cut 1½ inches thick
3 tablespoons butter or margarine
3 tablespoons olive or salad oil
½ teaspoon dried dillweed
1 cup dry white wine

¼ cup lemon juice
½ pound mushrooms sliced thin
8 lemon slices
Salt and pepper
2 teaspoons chopped parsley

1. In a good-sized heavy skillet melt the butter and combine with oil and dillweed. With paper towels wipe the salmon steaks dry and lay them in the skillet. Sauté them over medium heat about 5 minutes. Using 2 spatulas, turn them over.

2. Add the wine, lemon juice, and mushrooms to the skillet. Cover and simmer 5 minutes longer. Add the lemon slices, season to taste, cover again, and simmer another 5 minutes.

3. Lift the steaks to a hot platter, using 2 spatulas to keep them whole. Turn the heat up under the skillet and boil the sauce hard for 5 minutes to reduce it somewhat. Pour over the salmon. Sprinkle with chopped parsley. *Serves 4.*

Serve with macaroni salad (see Index) and buttered asparagus.

FILLET OF SOLE ROLLS WITH PEAS

1½ pounds fillet of sole
   Salt and pepper
2 tablespoons lemon juice
¼ cup dry white wine
3 tablespoons butter or
   margarine
1 tablespoon flour

½ cup chicken broth
1 cup canned tomatoes or 2
   medium tomatoes peeled and
   chopped
½ can tiny boiled onions
1 package frozen peas cooked
   Paprika

1. Cut the fish into strips about 2 inches wide and 4–5 inches long. Roll up the pieces and fasten with a toothpick. Lay them in a well-greased casserole, seam side down. Season, sprinkle with lemon juice and wine, and bake 10 minutes in a hot oven, 400°.
2. Melt the butter in a saucepan, stir in the flour, and gradually blend in the chicken broth. Drain the liquid from the casserole when the fish is ready and add to the sauce. Season to taste and stir in tomatoes.
3. Arrange the onions and peas over the fish rolls, pour the sauce over all, sprinkle with paprika, and return to the oven for another 10 minutes. *Serves 4–5.*

Serve with buttered corn on the cob and tomato-egg mold (see Index).

GREEK SKEWERED SWORDFISH

2 pounds swordfish sliced 1-inch
   thick and cut in 1-inch cubes
¼ cup lemon juice
2 tablespoons salad oil
1 teaspoon salt

Pepper
1 tablespoon chopped parsley
Bay leaves
Olive or salad oil

1. Mix the lemon juice, oil, salt, pepper, and parsley and stir the swordfish cubes well in the mixture. Let them marinate at least 1 hour.
2. Drain the swordfish and string the cubes on skewers, with a small piece of bay leaf between each two cubes.

3. Brush the fish lightly with oil and broil about 8-10 minutes, or until it is golden brown. Or broil it over charcoal on an outdoor grill. 4. Serve sprinkled with parsley and with lemon wedges. Or make a dressing of 3 tablespoons each of oil and lemon juice, 1 tablespoon chopped parsley, and salt and pepper to taste, and drizzle this over the swordfish. *Serves 5–6.*

Serve with buttered asparagus and a jellied lime-melon salad (see Index).

BAKED SWORDFISH

1¾-pound slice of swordfish	2 scallions minced (green onions)
¾ cup olive or salad oil	½ teaspoon orégano
½ clove garlic mashed	Salt and pepper

Mix well all ingredients except fish. Lay the swordfish in a baking dish or casserole just slightly larger than the fish and pour the sauce over. Let stand at room temperature at least 2 hours and then bake 30–40 minutes in a 350° oven, or until tender. *Serves 6.*

Serve with a macaroni salad and green beans almondine (see Index).

NEW ENGLAND BAKED SWORDFISH

LAY a swordfish steak about 1½ inches thick and weighing about 1½ pounds in a shallow casserole or baking pan. Pour in top milk or thin cream to a depth of half the thickness of the fish. Salt and pepper the fish and dot with butter. Bake 30 minutes in a 375° oven, basting occasionally. The milk should be largely absorbed and the fish brown but moist. *Serves 4–5.*

Serve with Gruyère potatoes and zucchini pierette (see Index).

SWORDFISH STEAK

1 slice swordfish 1 inch thick
¼ cup butter or margarine
½ teaspoon curry powder (scant)

½ cup finely minced onion
1 tablespoon lemon juice
Salt and pepper

THIS is an exceptionally flavorful way to cook swordfish.

1. Melt the butter in a small saucepan and stir in the curry powder, onion, lemon juice, and salt and pepper to taste.
2. Spread half of mixture over one side of the swordfish and broil about 4 inches from the heat for 7–8 minutes, or until golden brown.
3. Turn the steak, spread with the rest of the sauce, and broil the second side of the steak. *Serves 3–4.*

Serve with potato salad and green succotash (see Index), as well as a tossed salad.

TUNA-BROCCOLI CASSEROLE

7-ounce can tuna fish drained and
   flaked
2 pounds broccoli closely trimmed
   or 2 packages frozen
4 tablespoons butter or margarine
4 tablespoons flour

1 cup light cream
1 cup chicken broth
   Salt and pepper to taste
1 tablespoon chopped parsley
2 hard-boiled eggs sliced
¼ cup grated Parmesan cheese

1. Cook the broccoli, trimmed to remove most of the stems and leaves, until barely tender. Arrange in a single layer in a greased shallow casserole.
2. Melt the butter in a saucepan and make a cream sauce with the flour, cream, and chicken broth. Season to taste and stir in the parsley, tuna, and eggs.
3. Pour the tuna sauce gently over the broccoli and top with the

cheese. Bake 15–20 minutes in a medium oven, 375°, and brown a moment under the broiler. *Serves 6.*

Serve with a Swiss cheese and potato salad (see Index) and a tossed salad.

TUNA FLORENTINE

7-ounce can solid-pack tuna fish
1 package frozen chopped spinach
½ teaspoon margarine or oil
    Salt and pepper to taste
    Nutmeg
3-ounce can sliced mushrooms with liquid
2 tablespoons lemon juice
    Water or dry white wine

3 tablespoons butter or margarine
1 tablespoon minced onion
2 tablespoons flour
½ teaspoon salt
⅛ teaspoon pepper
1 small bay leaf crushed
1 egg slightly beaten
1 tablespoon grated Parmesan cheese

1. Thaw the spinach in a minute amount of margarine or oil (not more than ½ teaspoon) over the lowest possible heat, turning the block often. Press out as much liquid as possible with a spatula and season the spinach to taste with salt and pepper and a good pinch of nutmeg. Arrange it in a 1½-quart casserole, rather shallow.
2. Drain the oil from the tuna if it is packed in oil, put the tuna in a sieve, and rinse it well under running water.
3. Drain the liquid from the mushrooms and combine it with the lemon juice, adding enough water or white wine to make 1 cup.
4. In a small skillet melt 2 tablespoons of the butter, blend in the onion and flour, salt, pepper, and bay leaf. Cook until thick and beat in the egg. Stir in the mushrooms.
5. Arrange the tuna fish in good-sized hunks on top of the spinach and pour the sauce over. Dot with the remaining tablespoon of butter and sprinkle with cheese. *Serves 6.*

Serve with oven-crisped French-fried potato sticks and quick tomato aspic ring mold (see Index).

CHINESE TUNA CASSEROLE

7-ounce can solid-pack tuna fish
1 can condensed cream of mushroom soup
⅓ cup milk, chicken broth, or water
3-ounce can Chinese noodles

1 cup sliced celery
½ cup whole salted cashew nuts
¼ cup minced onion
Salt and pepper to taste

COMBINE all the ingredients, reserving 1 cup of the noodles, and stir gently until well bended. Spread in a shallow 1-quart casserole. Bake in a moderate oven, 350°, 20 minutes. Spread the remaining noodles over the top and bake 5 minutes longer. *Serves 4–5.*

Serve with a vegetable salad (see Index) and a tossed salad.

QUICK TUNA LUNCHEON CASSEROLE

2 seven-ounce cans tuna fish
  drained and coarsely broken up
1 small onion chopped
½ cup diced green pepper
2 tablespoons butter or margarine
2 tablespoons flour
1 teaspoon salt
¼ teaspoon pepper

¼ teaspoon dried thyme or
  rosemary or ¾ teaspoon fresh
4-ounce can sliced mushrooms
1 cup evaporated milk
1 tablespoon Worcestershire sauce
4-ounce can whole-kernel corn or
  ½ cup fresh-cooked corn
4-ounce can potato sticks

1. Sauté the onion and green pepper lightly in the butter, and blend in the flour, salt, pepper, and thyme or rosemary. Stir in slowly the liquid drained from the mushrooms, mixed with the evaporated milk. Stir constantly until it comes to a boil.
2. Add the Worcestershire sauce, corn, mushrooms, and tuna. Turn into a small casserole and top with the potato sticks. Bake in a 375° oven 20 minutes, or until it is bubbly. *Serves 4–6.*

Serve with bean salad (see Index) and a green salad.

DEVILED CRAB

1 pound crabmeat carefully flaked and broken into chunks
1 tablespoon butter or margarine
2 tablespoons chopped onion
1 tablespoon chopped green pepper
½ teaspoon salt
Dash cayenne pepper
1 teaspoon prepared mustard
2 cups fairly thick cream sauce
2 egg yolks
¼ cup light cream
1 tablespoon chopped chives
1 tablespoon chopped parsley
½ teaspoon Worcestershire sauce
Buttered crumbs

1. Melt the butter in a saucepan and cook the onion and green pepper until tender. Add salt, pepper, and mustard.
2. Make the cream sauce with 3 tablespoons butter or margarine, 3 tablespoons flour, 2 cups milk, and salt and pepper to taste. Stir into the hot sauce the egg yolks beaten with the cream.
3. Stir in the chives, Worcestershire sauce, parsley, cooked onion and green pepper, and then blend in gently the crabmeat. Spread out in a shallow buttered casserole and top with buttered crumbs.
4. Bake in a 350° oven 35 minutes, or until golden brown. Or bake half that time, then place under the broiler until brown and bubbling. *Serves 4.*

Serve with blender avocado ring mold salad (see Index) and a plate of sliced tomatoes, each slice topped with a dab of French dressing mixed with fresh chopped herbs.

CRAB MORNAY

THIS is practically a classic luncheon dish, and there are many recipes for it. In general, this is the way to make it, in individual casseroles or in one larger shallow casserole. Build up as follows per person:

1. A thin layer of rich white sauce, quite thick
2. ½ cup picked-over lump crabmeat
3. ½ cup white sauce mixed with ½ tablespoon sherry
4. Thin slice Cheddar cheese
5. Melted butter and a dash of paprika

Bake 10 minutes at 350°.

Serve with potato salad and guacamole mold (see Index), together with a tossed green salad and dinner rolls.

CRAB IMPERIAL

1 cup crabmeat picked over and
  flaked, fresh, frozen, or canned
1 tablespoon butter or margarine
1 tablespoon flour
½ teaspoon dry mustard
¼ teaspoon salt
⅛ teaspoon paprika
1 cup milk
1 egg yolk
1 tablespoon sherry

THIS is a good way of making another classic crab dish.

1. Make a cream sauce of the butter, flour, mustard, salt, and paprika. Cook for a moment and stir in ¾ cup of the milk, continuing to stir until it is smooth and thickened. Season to taste.

2. Beat the egg yolk with the remaining ¼ cup milk, and then with a little of the hot cream sauce. Add all at once to the rest of the cream sauce and simmer 5 minutes, stirring frequently.

3. Add the crabmeat and the sherry to the sauce, check seasoning, and serve on fresh hot toast or in patty shells or over rice. *Serves 3–4.*

Serve with a molded vegetable salad (see Index) and a plain tossed green salad, together with warm garlic bread.

ORIENTAL CRAB WITH CASHEW NUTS

1 cup crabmeat flaked coarsely and
  picked over, fresh, frozen, or
  canned
1 can Chinese noodles
1 can condensed cream of mushroom soup
½ cup chopped celery
¼ cup whole cashew nuts
1 teaspoon minced onion
Salt and pepper to taste

1. Take out ½ cup of the noodles for use later as topping, and mix the rest of the noodles with the soup, celery, nuts, onion, and crabmeat.

2. When thoroughly blended, arrange in a buttered casserole and bake 20 minutes in a 350° oven. Add the remaining noodles for topping, and bake 5 minutes more. *Serves 3–4.*

Serve with a grapefruit ring mold and a mixed vegetable salad (see Index).

QUICK CRAB NEWBURG

1½ cups crabmeat picked over and coarsely flaked, canned, fresh, or frozen
1 can condensed cream of mush-room soup

4 tablespoons cream
2 tablespoons sherry
Dash nutmeg

THIS is one of the most popular ways to fix crabmeat. Stir all the ingredients together gently, heat almost to the boiling point, and serve on freshly made toast, fluffy hot rice, or in scrubbed crab shells. *Serves 4.*

Serve with a peach-cheese ring and coleslaw (see Index).

CRAB TETRAZZINI

½ pound crabmeat picked over and flaked, fresh, frozen, or canned
½ teaspoon minced shallots
2 tablespoons butter or margarine
¼ teaspoon paprika
1 tablespoon melted butter or margarine

1 tablespoon floor
1 cup light cream
1 tablespoon dry sherry
Salt and pepper
1 egg yolk slightly beaten
2 tablespoons grated Parmesan cheese

1. Lightly sauté the crabmeat and the shallots in the butter, and stir in the paprika.
2. In a saucepan make a cream sauce with the melted butter, flour, and cream. Add the sherry and season to taste.
3. Remove the saucepan from the heat for a moment and stir in the egg yolk rapidly, stirring until the sauce is thick and smooth.
4. Combine the sauce with the crabmeat and pour over fresh-cooked rice or noodles or spaghetti. Sprinkle with the Parmesan cheese and brown under the broiler. *Serves 4–6.*

Serve with a tomato-egg mold and Italian green beans with water chestnuts (see Index).

GRILLED ROCK LOBSTER

FOR 4 rock lobster tails make a sauce of ½ cup melted butter or margarine, 1 small clove garlic crushed, ½ teaspoon salt, ½ teaspoon pepper, and ¼ cup lemon juice.

Split the tails the full length on the underside, about ⅔ of the way through. Grill about 3 inches from the flame, first 8 minutes on the shell side and then 6 minutes on the cut side. Keep basting the cut side while that is broiling. Serve 1 tail per person.

Serve with potato salad and coleslaw and a platter of sliced tomatoes.

LOBSTER QUICHE

1 pound fresh lobster meat cut up
  in good-sized chunks
  Pastry for 9-inch pie plate
3 tablespoons butter or margarine
  Salt and pepper
3 tablespoons dry sherry or
  Maderia
4 eggs

1 tablespoon flour
½ teaspoon salt
  Few grains cayenne pepper
2 cups light cream
1 tablespoon melted butter or
  margarine
  Grated Parmesan cheese

1. Roll out pastry and line a 9-inch pie plate.
2. Melt the butter in a skillet and when it is sizzling add the lobster meat. Sauté lightly 2–3 minutes. Sprinkle lightly with salt and pepper, stir in the sherry or Madeira, cover, and simmer over very low heat 3–4 minutes. Pour into the pie shell, with all the juice.
3. Beat together the eggs, flour, the ½ teaspoon salt, and cayenne. Stir in the cream and melted butter, pour over the lobster, top with cheese, and bake in a moderate oven, 375°, about 40 minutes, or until the custard is firm and the top golden brown. *Serves 6.*

Serve with an avocado mousse (see Index) and a large mixed vegetable salad.

CHINESE SHRIMP CASSEROLE

¾ pound cleaned and cooked small shrimp
½ cup chopped celery
1 cup chopped onion
½ cup water
4-ounce can sliced mushrooms
2 tablespoons butter or margarine
¾ cup chopped green pepper
6-ounce can cashew nuts chopped
4-ounce can pimiento drained and chopped
5-ounce can water chestnuts sliced
2½ cups medium cream sauce
Salt and pepper
2 three-ounce cans Chinese noodles

1. Put the celery and onion in a saucepan with the water and simmer until the onion is soft. Drain.
2. Sauté the mushrooms lightly in the butter. Stir in the onion-celery mixture, green pepper, cashews, pimiento, water chestnuts, and shrimp.
3. Make the cream sauce of 3½ tablespoons butter or margarine, 3½ tablespoons flour, and 2½ cups milk. Season to taste and stir into the shrimp mixture.
4. Spread 1 can of noodles on the bottom of a good-sized casserole, cover it with the shrimp-sauce mixture, and top with the other can of noodles. Bake 30 minutes in a 350° oven. *Serves 8–10.*

Serve with Chinese vegetable salad and a plate of sliced tomatoes.

# SALADS

Since hot weather is the prime time for making salad a part of the menu, for lunch or dinner or both, this is the longest section of the cookbook. The salads in the first section all have as their principal ingredient cold meat, chicken, crabmeat, shrimp, lobster, ham, tongue, cold cuts, or some other substantial food. They all make delicious and substantial eating, and should play a real role in summer cookery.

In the second section are salads of all kinds, from the simplest tossed green salad to fruit salads, vegetable salads, molded salads and combination salads that form the principal part of the meal.

MAIN COURSE SALADS

SALADE BOULANGÈRE

1½ cups diced cooked potatoes
3 cups diced cooked beef, chicken, or turkey
1 cup cut-up cooked green beans
1 cup watercress, stems removed, coarsely shredded

6 radishes sliced (unpeeled)
2 tablespoons chopped scallions (green onions) or onions
1 cup chili sauce
¼ cup mayonnaise
¼ cup wine vinegar

THIS good hearty salad provides the major part of a meal.
1. Combine the potatoes, meat, beans, watercress, radishes, and scallions in a serving bowl.
2. Mix together the chili sauce, mayonnaise, and vinegar. Pour over the salad and toss until well blended. *Serves 6.*

Serve with a plate of sliced tomatoes, each slice topped with a little French dressing mixed with fresh chopped herbs; tarragon, basil, orégano, dill, thyme, and parsley.

QUICK AND EASY CHEF'S SALAD

1 quart mixed greens, washed,
dried, torn up, and chilled
2 cups julienned smoked tongue,
cold roast beef, corned beef,
ham, chicken, or turkey, or any
mixture of them

¼ pound Swiss cheese julienned
2 tablespoons chopped parsley
French dressing

CHEF'S salad is a staple everywhere, and can be made with almost any kind of cold meat or poultry, or both, and with many kinds of cheese. A pleasant variation is to rub a slice of stale white bread vigorously with a cut clove of garlic, cut it into small dice, and toss with the remaining ingredients.

Have all the ingredients chilled well and toss together in a large salad bowl, until everything is well coated with dressing. Serve at once. *Serves 4–5.*

Serve with baked sliced Idahos (see Index) and a platter of sliced tomatoes, celery sticks, carrot sticks, and radish roses, with a side dish of French dressing.

CORNED-BEEF SALAD

4 medium potatoes cooked, diced,
and chilled
12-ounce can corned beef diced
2 small dill pickles diced
½ cup diced celery
1 small onion chopped

French dressing
2 tablespoons lemon juice
2 teaspoons prepared mustard
1 tablespoon Worcestershire sauce
1 teaspoon salt

1. Combine the potatoes and corned beef and stir in the pickles, celery, and onion. Toss lightly.
2. Combine French dressing (about ¾ cup) with lemon juice, mustard, Worcestershire sauce, and salt if corned beef is not salty enough.
3. Pour the dressing over the meat-potato mixture, stir well but carefully, cover, chill at least an hour. Serve on crisp lettuce. *Serves 4–6.*

Serve with quick scalloped potatoes, jellied pear salad (see Index), and hot rolls.

PLAIN CHICKEN SALAD

3 cups cooked chicken cut in ¾-inch   Mayonnaise
   dice, mostly white meat   Capers
3 cups diced celery   Hard-cooked eggs
1 cup shredded lettuce   Tomatoes cut in wedges

CHICKEN salad and potato salad run a close race for the most popular American salad, and this explains why so many variations of chicken salad are given here.

1. Blend the chicken, celery, lettuce, and mayonnaise well in a bowl. Arrange on a lettuce-lined platter or bowl, garnish with capers, and put wedges of hard-cooked eggs and tomatoes around the edge. *Serves 5–6.*

Serve with a casserole of macaroni and cheese and warm garlic bread.

ALMOND CHICKEN SALAD

3 cups cooked chicken cut in dice,   ⅓ cup seedless white grapes (cut
   mostly white meat   in 2 if large)
⅔ cup chopped sweet pickles   ½ cup mayonnaise
½ cup blanched, slivered, toasted   ½ teaspoon salt
   almonds   1½ teaspoons vinegar

1. Mix together the chicken, pickles, almonds, and grapes.
2. Blend the mayonnaise, salt, and vinegar.
3. Stir the dressing into the chicken mixture and toss lightly. Chill.
4. Serve the salad in lettuce cups and garnish with watercress, stems removed. *Serves 4–6.*

Note: A pleasant alternative to the almonds is thinly sliced water chestnuts, which give a crisp quality to the salad.

Serve with parsley-buttered little new potatoes and a platter of cold vegetables, such as sliced or quartered tomatoes, celery and carrot sticks, cucumber fingers, etc., and warm garlic bread.

CHICKEN-HAM SALAD MEAL

1 cup cooked chicken cut in small dice
1 cup julienned cooked ham
8 anchovy fillets chopped
¼ pound medium cooked hot Spanish or Italian sausage sliced thin
3 cold boiled potatoes diced small
1 green pepper sliced thin
2 heads Belgian endive sliced thin
¼ cup chopped scallions, including the green part (green onions)
6 stuffed olives sliced
6 ripe olives chopped
¼ cup chopped parsley
French dressing flavored with garlic
3 hard-cooked eggs shelled and chilled

1. Gently mix, in a large bowl, all of the ingredients except the eggs.
2. Remove the yolks from the eggs and chop the whites coarsely to add to the salad. Mound the salad on a serving platter lined with crisp lettuce.
3. Sieve the egg yolks over the ready-to-serve salad. Garnish with little cherry tomatoes and radish roses. *Serves 8.*

Serve with quick green bean casserole (see Index) and French-fried potatoes, together with hot rolls, cornbread, corn muffins, or blueberry muffins.

TOKAY CHICKEN SALAD

1½ cups cooked chicken diced coarsely
1 cup Tokay grapes, halved and seeded, and extra small bunches for garnish
¼ cup mayonnaise
2 tablespoons chopped almonds
2 tablespoons lemon juice
2 teaspoons instant minced onion
½ teaspoon salt
Dash pepper

STIR together the chicken, halved grapes, mayonnaise, almonds, lemon juice, minced onion, salt and pepper. Chill well. Serve in lettuce cups and garnish with small bunches Tokay grapes. *Serves 4.*

Serve with a hot rice casserole and a plate of sliced or quartered tomatoes, carrot sticks, cucumber fingers, and celery sticks.

CHICKEN SALAD WITH FRUIT

2 cups cooked chicken or 2 six-
ounce cans, chilled and
coarsely cut up
1 head Boston or leaf lettuce
½ head romaine
1 cup thinly sliced celery
8¾-ounce can pineapple tidbits
drained

¼ cup French dressing
¼ cup mayonnaise
3 fresh peaches peeled and halved
or 1 can cling-style halves
Small bunches seedless green
grapes
3 tablespoons toasted slivered
almonds

1. Save the outer leaves of the lettuce and romaine to line the serving bowl, and break the rest up into a large bowl.
2. Add to the bowl the celery, chicken, ½ cup of the pineapple, and stir well with the French dressing and mayonnaise blended. Chill.
3. At serving time line the serving bowl with the reserved lettuce and romaine leaves and pile in the salad.
4. Arrange the peach halves around the edge of the bowl, cut side up. Fill the peach hollows with the rest of the pineapple and top each with a small bunch of grapes. Sprinkle the almonds over the salad. *Serves 4.*

Serve with molded fruit salad with ginger (see Index) and a hot casserole of potatoes, macaroni, spoon bread, or noodles.

CRAB-AVOCADO SALAD

6 ounces crabmeat, canned, fresh,
or frozen, coarsely flaked
½ cup catsup
3 tablespoons lemon juice

Dash Tabasco
Salt and pepper
2 medium avocados split and
pitted

1. Mix the catsup, lemon juice, Tabasco, and season to taste.
2. Mix the dressing lightly with the crabmeat and pile in the avocado halves. *Serves 4.*

Serve with asparagus-cheese soufflé and jellied pear salad (see Index).

92

CRABMEAT SALAD

1 cup coarsely flaked crabmeat, fresh, canned, or frozen
2 hard-cooked eggs chopped
1 cup chopped celery
½ teaspoon salt

2 tablespoons slivered, toasted almonds
½ cup mayonnaise
2 tablespoons vinegar

1. Mix the crabmeat, carefully picked over, with the chopped eggs, celery, salt, and almonds. Chill.
2. Blend the mayonnaise and vinegar and combine with the crabmeat mixture. Garnish with tomato wedges and additional hard-cooked eggs cut in wedges. *Serves 4.*

Serve with spaghetti and cheese and golden salad (see Index).

MOLDED CRABMEAT SALAD

2 cups coarsely flaked crabmeat, canned, fresh, or frozen
2 envelopes gelatin
1 cup cold water
½ teaspoon salt

¼ cup lemon juice
2 cups mayonnaise
2 teaspoons instant minced onion
1 cup chopped celery

1. Soften gelatin in the water and heat slowly until dissolved, stirring constantly. Beat in the salt, lemon juice, mayonnaise, and onion. Chill until it begins to thicken.
2. Fold in celery and crabmeat and pour into small mold. A fish mold is especially suitable. Chill until firm.
3. Unmold on chilled platter and garnish with additional chunks of crabmeat, strips of pimiento, and salad greens. *Serves 6–8.*

Serve with blender avocado ring salad (see Index), filled with creamed mushrooms, and a plate of cut-up tomatoes, celery and carrot sticks, and either cucumber fingers or cucumbers in sour cream (see Index).

HAM AND POTATO SALAD RING

I. 1½ cups chopped or ground
    ham
   1 envelope plain gelatin
   ½ cup water
   2 tablespoons minced onion
   ½ cup mayonnaise
   ½ cup chili sauce
   1 teaspoon prepared horse-
    radish
   2 teaspoons prepared
    mustard
   ¼ teaspoon Tabasco sauce

II. 2 cups cooked and diced
    potatoes
   1 envelope plain gelatin
   ½ cup water
   1 cup diced celery
   1 small onion minced
   2 tablespoons green pepper
    minced
   ½ cup mayonnaise
   1 tablespoon vinegar
   1¼ teaspoon salt
   ⅛ teaspoon fresh-ground
    pepper

I. In Part I, sprinkle the gelatin on the water, dissolve over low heat, remove from heat and stir in remaining ingredients in Part I. Turn into a medium ring mold and chill until almost firm.

II. Prepare Part II the same way as Part I. Dissolve the gelatin first, remove from the heat and stir in all remaining ingredients in Part II. Pour over the almost firm Part I and chill until set.

Unmold on a chilled platter and garnish with salad greens and tomato wedges. *Serves 8.*

Serve with spaghetti with tomato sauce and Italian green beans with water chestnuts (see Index).

HAWAIIAN LUNCHEON MEAT SALAD

12-ounce can luncheon meat
¼ cup mayonnaise
¼ cup dairy sour cream

8¾-ounce can crushed pineapple
3 cups finely shredded cabbage
¼ cup thinly sliced carrots

1. Slice the block of meat into 8 crosswise pieces, and cut each slice in 12 pieces.
2. Blend the mayonnaise, sour cream, and 1 tablespoon of the juice from the pineapple.
3. Drain the pineapple well and combine it with the meat, cabbage, and carrots.
4. Toss the mixture lightly with the mayonnaise mixture. Chill at least 1 hour. *Serves 4–6.*

Serve with cheese ring with vegetable salad (see Index) and hot muffins.

TONGUE AND POTATO SALAD MEAL

2 cups sliced cooked potatoes	1 teaspoon salt
2 cups diced tongue (canned)	⅛ teaspoon fresh-ground black
1½ cups sliced fresh mushrooms	pepper
4 tablespoons salad oil	¼ cup shredded raw carrots
4 tablespoons lemon juice	½ cup chopped celery
¼ cup minced onion or shallots	2 hard-cooked eggs sliced

1. Sauté the mushrooms lightly in the oil. Cool somewhat.
2. Add the lemon juice, onion, salt and pepper, and let stand until cold.
3. Mix the potatoes, carrots, celery, and tongue.
4. Pour the mushroom mixture over the potato mixture, mix well, and let marinate at least an hour.
5. Spread the salad on a bed of lettuce on a large plate, and arrange the egg slices on top. Serve with mayonnaise. *Serves 6.*

Serve with molded grapefruit-avocado salad (see Index) and hot muffins.

DANISH SALMON SALAD

7¾-ounce can salmon, drained and
    coarsely flaked
1 medium tomato peeled and
    chopped
½ small cucumber peeled and
    diced

½ teaspoon salt
    Grind of pepper
2 tablespoons French dressing
3 tablespoons dairy sour cream
1 teaspoon dried dillweed

Mix together the salmon, tomato, cucumber, and salt and pepper to taste. Blend the French dressing with the sour cream, add the dill-weed, and combine everything. Chill well. *Serves 3–4.*

Serve with a Greek salad platter and hot rolls.

SHRIMP AND AVOCADO VINAIGRETTE

2 medium avocados cut in half
    and pitted
1 pound cooked shrimp, shelled
    and cleaned
¼ teaspoon salt
    Dash fresh-ground black pepper

⅛ teaspoon garlic powder
⅛ teaspoon dry mustard
¼ cup salad oil
2 tablespoons wine vinegar
1 tablespoon grated onion

1. Scoop out the pulp of the avocados and cut up coarsely. Save the shells.
2. Chop the shrimp coarsely and combine with the avocados.
3. Shake together vigorously the salt, pepper, garlic powder, mustard, oil, vinegar, and onion. Pour over the shrimp-avocado mixture and blend well but carefully. Chill at least 1 hour.
4. Pour the salad into the avocado shells and serve. *Serves 4.*

Serve with salade niçoise (see Index), sliced tomatoes, and corn on the cob.

96

SHRIMP AND CRABMEAT SALAD

1 pound shrimp cooked, shelled, and cleaned
½ pound crabmeat coarsely flaked, canned, fresh, or frozen
½ cup mayonnaise
¼ cup French dressing

2 tablespoons lemon juice
1 tablespoon minced parsley
1 tablespoon minced onion or shallots
Salt and pepper

1. Blend the mayonnaise, French dressing, lemon juice, parsley, onion, and salt and pepper to taste.
2. Mix the shrimp (cut in two if large) and crabmeat, and blend carefully but well with the dressing. Chill well. *Serves 4–5.*

Serve with cottage cheese, deviled eggs, buttered fresh asparagus, and hot garlic bread.

TURKEY BUFFET SALAD

2 quarts cut-up cooked turkey (2½-3 pounds, mostly breast meat)
20-ounce can water chestnuts sliced
2 pounds seedless grapes
2 cups sliced celery
2 cups toasted slivered blanched almonds

1 teaspoon curry powder or more to taste
2 tablespoons soy sauce
3 cups mayonnaise
1-pound-13-ounce can pineapple chunks

1. Cut the turkey into bite-size pieces, not too small. Stir in the water chestnuts, washed and stemmed grapes, celery, and 1½ cups of the almonds.
2. Mix the curry powder and soy sauce with the mayonnaise, and combine with the turkey mixture. Mix well and chill for several hours. Top with remaining nuts.
3. Spoon into lettuce cups, and distribute the pineapple chunks on top of the salad. *Serves 12 generously.*

Serve with a platter of sliced ripe tomatoes, each slice topped with a little French dressing mixed with mixed fresh herbs. Wilted cucumbers blended with sour cream and hot garlic bread or rolls go well, too.

TUNA-POTATO SALAD

1 large tin tuna drained and broken up
2 heads romaine (heart leaves only)
1 head curly endive (chicory)
1 large bunch watercress destemmed

4 small cooked potatoes sliced
1 green pepper seeded and julienned
3 small tomatoes cut in wedges
French dressing

1. Wash the greens and dry well. Cut in bite-size pieces, about one inch.
2. Put greens in large bowl and add tuna, potatoes, green pepper, and tomatoes. Chill well.
3. At serving time toss lightly with just enough French dressing to moisten all ingredients well. *Serves 6–8.*

Serve with a macaroni and cheese casserole and warm garlic bread.

VEGETABLE–COLD-CUT SALAD

1 cup cooked lima beans
½ cup raw shredded carrot
½ cup diced cooked potatoes
2 tablespoons minced onion
1 medium cucumber peeled and diced
⅓ cup French dressing

1 cup mixed cold cuts cut in julienne strips
2 hard-cooked eggs chopped
1 dill pickle chopped
3 tablespoons lemon juice or vinegar
½ cup mayonnaise
Salt and pepper to taste

1. Mix the lima beans, carrot, potatoes, onion, and cucumber with the French dressing and marinate, in the refrigerator, at least ½ hour.
2. Stir in the cold cuts, eggs, and pickle.
3. At serving time add the lemon juice to the mayonnaise and combine with the chilled salad. Correct seasoning. Serve on lettuce leaves. *Serves 5–6.*

Serve with buttered corn on the cob and hot rolls.

GREEN SALADS

SIMPLE TOSSED GREEN SALAD

Mixed greens

French Dressing

1 cup salad oil or half olive oil
¼ cup wine vinegar or lemon juice

1 teaspoon mixed dried herbs or
1 tablespoon fresh, chopped
1 scant teaspoon salt
Fresh-ground black pepper to
taste

MIXED greens make the best salad, and it is easy to have an assortment: leaf or Boston lettuce, iceberg lettuce, Bibb lettuce, salad-bowl lettuce, chicory, endive, romaine. Tear them up, making sure that they are well washed, dried, and crisped. Mix the dressing in a jar and shake it well. Pour over just enough to coat each piece of greens, with no leftover pool of dressing in the bottom of the bowl. Toss the salad well, until it barely begins to wilt a bit. As the French describe it, the salad should *"se fatigue."*

DUTCH LETTUCE

1 head lettuce shredded
3 slices bacon cut in small strips
2 tablespoons chopped onion

1 scant tablespoon flour
2 tablespoons mild vinegar
Salt and pepper

1. Sauté the bacon until crisp. Skim out and add to the lettuce.
2. Sauté the onion lightly in the bacon fat. Stir in the flour and blend.
3. Stir the vinegar into this mixture. If the vinegar is rather sharp dilute it with a little water. Stir until smooth, season to taste, and pour over the lettuce. Toss well, until the lettuce is a little wilted, and serve at once, while still warm. This is the so-called "wilted lettuce" liked by so many people. *Serves 4.*

GOURMET CAESAR SALAD

3 medium heads washed and dried
romaine broken into bite-size
pieces
1 cup hot croutons
Garlic
Salt
5 fillets of anchovies mashed to a
paste

4 tablespoons garlic-flavored oil,
preferably at least half olive oil
Few drops Worcestershire sauce
Fresh-ground black pepper
1-minute coddled egg
3 tablespoons grated Parmesan
cheese
2 lemons

CAESAR salad is a nationwide favorite, and is not too difficult to make. It should properly be made at the table, as its preparation is a fascinating ritual.

1. Prepare the croutons before beginning to mix the salad. Cut 2 slices of bread, crusts removed, into 16 cubes each. Sauté them delicately in oil well scented with garlic.

2. Have a large wooden bowl, well rubbed with a cut clove of garlic, ready, with the romaine in it.

3. Pour over the greens the mashed anchovies and garlic-flavored oil, the Worcestershire sauce, a good grinding of pepper, the coddled egg, and the Parmesan cheese. Salt lightly.

4. Have the lemons cut in two and squeeze them hard directly over the greens.

5. Toss the salad lightly but thoroughly. Every trace of the egg should disappear.

6. Add the hot croutons and toss again until they are well mixed into the salad. *This should make 4 large portions as a separate course, or it will serve 6 as a side dish.*

CABBAGE SALADS

DUTCH KOOLSLAA

½ cup dairy sour cream
1 teaspoon salt
2 teaspoons sugar
2 tablespoons vinegar
1 cup canned crushed pineapple
   drained

1 teaspoon caraway seeds
Dash paprika
2 cups green cabbage finely
   shredded and crisped in ice water

1. Blend the cream, salt, sugar, vinegar, pineapple, caraway seeds, and paprika. Chill at least 1 hour.
2. Drain the crisped cabbage well and blend it with the dressing. *Serves 6.*

FRUIT COLESLAW

1 head cabbage finely shredded
   and crisped in ice water
1 cup diced pineapple, fresh or
   canned
½ cup green grapes cut in half
   and seeded
1 cup dairy sour cream

1 cup mayonnaise
3 tablespoons sugar
1 tablespoon lemon juice
1 teaspoon grated orange rind
   Shredded toasted blanched
   almonds

1. Combine the chilled cabbage with the pineapple and grapes.
2. Mix the sour cream, mayonnaise, sugar, lemon juice, and orange rind.
3. Toss the cabbage lightly but thoroughly with the dressing and mound on a platter. Sprinkle with almonds. Chill before serving. *Serves 6–8.*

MORAVIAN COLESLAW

1 head cabbage shredded or
   finely chopped
2 teaspoons salt
½ cup water
2½ tablespoons sugar
2 tablespoons salad oil

2 tablespoons vinegar
½ teaspoon ground caraway seeds
Pepper
1 cup dairy sour cream
Paprika

1. Sprinkle the cabbage with the salt, cover with wax paper, place a weight on it, and let stand 1 hour. Drain well.
2. Combine the water, sugar, oil, vinegar, caraway seeds, and pepper to taste. Blend well and stir into the cabbage.
3. Fold in the sour cream and sprinkle well with paprika. *Serves 6.*

VEGETABLE SALADS

FRESH ASPARAGUS SALAD

2 pounds fresh asparagus cooked
1 small head iceberg lettuce broken
   into small pieces
   French dressing
2 tomatoes sliced in thin wedges

1 small cucumber peeled and sliced
3 scallions sliced thin (green
   onions)
2 hard-cooked eggs sliced
½ cup sliced ripe olives

1. Toss the lettuce with a little French dressing and spread it out in a wide bowl or on a deep plate.
2. Put little bunches of 3–4 spears of asparagus all around the outside of the lettuce, with groups of 3–4 wedges of tomato between.
3. Insert the cucumber slices over and between the asparagus and tomatoes.
4. Sprinkle the sliced scallions over everything.
5. Arrange the egg slices in a small circle in the center of the plate. Sprinkle the ripe olives over the eggs.
6. Drizzle French dressing lightly over the entire platter and serve with more dressing. *Serves 5.*

AVOCADO SALAD I

3 medium avocados sliced
1 clove garlic
6 hard-cooked eggs sliced
¾ cup Roquefort cheese coarsely
  grated

2 small heads iceberg lettuce
  shredded
French dressing

AVOCADO is one of the most popular salad materials, and lends itself to many delightful combinations.
1. Rub a large bowl well with the cut surface of the garlic clove.
2. Combine the remaining ingredients and toss gently but thoroughly with your favorite French dressing. *Serves 8–10.*

AVOCADO SALAD II

WASH a ripe avocado. Halve it lengthwise and remove the seed. Scoop the meat from the shell with a ball cutter or a teaspoon. Combine the avocado balls with an equal quantity of pineapple chunks, fresh or canned, and moisten with French dressing. Spoon back into the shells and serve with more French dressing. *Serves 3–4.*

BEAN SALAD

1 package frozen cut wax beans
  cooked, or 1 can drained
1 package frozen cut green beans
  cooked or 1 can drained
15-ounce can kidney beans drained
  and rinsed

1 tablespoon Worcestershire sauce
8-ounce jar Italian-style salad
  dressing
¾ cup sweet pickle relish
½ cup sliced onion, preferably red
1 quart torn-up salad greens

THIS is a hearty and flavorful salad, a good item for a buffet meal or for the main dish of a summer luncheon.
1. Mix all the beans with the Worcestershire sauce and the dressing, season to taste, cover, and chill several hours.
2. When ready to serve, stir in the pickle, onion, and greens, and toss lightly but well. *Serves 8.*

STRING BEAN SALAD

2 packages frozen Frenched string
  beans cooked, or 1½ pounds
  fresh, cut and cooked
½ cup French dressing
¾ cup chopped onion

6 slices bacon cooked crisp and
  crumbled
6 hard-cooked eggs chopped
2 teaspoons minced parsley
⅓ cup mayonnaise
Salt to taste

1. The beans for this salad should be cooked until *barely* tender, so they are still a little crisp. Drain and cool them.
2. Mix with French dressing and onion, and chill until serving time.
3. When time to serve, mix with the crumbled bacon, chopped eggs, parsley, and mayonnaise, and season to taste. *Serves 6.*

SWEDISH BEAN SALAD

1 pound green beans cut in 1-inch
  lengths and cooked until barely
  tender
6 scallions chopped (green onions)

1 teaspoon chopped fresh dill or
  ½ teaspoon dried dillweed
1 teaspoon chopped parsley
  Salt and pepper to taste
⅓ cup mayonnaise

COMBINE ingredients, toss lightly, and chill. *Serves 4–5.*

CAULIFLOWER SALAD PROVENÇALE

1 large head cauliflower
20 pitted ripe olives, preferably
  Greek or Italian

3 canned sweet peppers cut in strips
  French dressing

1. Soak the cauliflower 30 minutes, head down, in salted water to cover. Break it up into separate flowerets and cook in boiling salted water 5–8 minutes. They should still be crisp. Drain well. Chill.
2. Combine the cooked and cooled cauliflower flowerets with the olives and peppers, toss with enough dressing to coat the pieces, and let marinate in the refrigerator several hours. Toss lightly before serving. *Serves 6.*

CREOLE SALAD

6 small zucchini cut in very thin
   slices diagonally (unpeeled)
3 tomatoes skinned and chopped
1 green pepper minced
1 avocado peeled and diced
2 scallions chopped

½ teaspoon sugar
1 teaspoon salt
¼ teaspoon fresh-ground pepper
2 cups torn-up romaine
   French dressing

Toss together all the ingredients except the dressing and chill 1 hour. At serving time toss with just enough French dressing to moisten all ingredients well. *Serves 6–8.*

ENDIVE SALAD WITH BEETS

1 pound Belgian endives cut in
   small pieces
½ pound cooked beets julienned

Salt and pepper to taste
2 tablespoons salad oil
Juice of 1 lemon

1. Wash and dry the endives. Cut in 1-inch pieces.
2. Toss with the beets, seasoning to taste, oil, and lemon juice. Garnish with parsley. *Serves 4–6.*

FARMER'S SALAD

2 cups diced cucumbers
1 cup diced radishes, unpeeled
½ cup red onions diced
½ pound diced American cheese

1 cup dairy sour cream
   Salt and pepper to taste
   Chopped fresh dill or dried
   dillseed to taste

Mix and season to taste. Add more sour cream if needed. *Serves 8.*

Serve with cold sliced roast beef, sliced tomatoes, and fresh corn on the cob.

SALADE NIÇOISE

COOK separately until barely tender equal parts of diced potatoes and cut green beans. Drain, chill, and combine with French dressing made with lemon juice instead of vinegar. Pile on a serving platter and garnish with black olives, capers, and wedges of peeled tomatoes.

CHINESE VEGETABLE SALAD

Salad
½ cup sliced water chestnuts (canned)
½ cup green pepper diced small
½ cup thinly-sliced celery
½ cup scallions thinly sliced (green onions)
½ cup bean sprouts (canned)
½ cup shredded Chinese cabbage Slivered toasted blanched almonds

Dressing
⅓ cup sesame-seed oil
2 tablespoons soy sauce
1 teaspoon prepared mustard
Juice 1 lemon or lime
Black pepper

1. Combine all the salad ingredients except the almonds.
2. Shake up the dressing ingredients in a jar.
3. Combine and toss lightly. Let mellow at least 10 minutes before serving. Sprinkle almonds on top before serving. *Serves 6.*

Serve with chow mein or with a platter of cold cuts and hot rolls.

DE LUXE VEGETABLE SALAD

1 pound cut green beans cooked until barely tender
1 pound new potatoes scraped and cooked until barely tender
¼ cup French dressing
2 tablespoons chopped onion

1 large or 2 medium ripe tomatoes diced
Lettuce leaves
Rolled anchovies with capers
1 tablespoon mixed fresh herbs (parsley, tarragon, basil, orégano)

106

1. Mix the beans and potatoes and blend with enough French dressing to moisten them well. If the potatoes are the little marble-sized ones, leave them whole. Otherwise cut up. (The tiny ones do not need to be either scraped or peeled.) Chill at least 1 hour.

2. When ready to serve toss lightly with onion and tomatoes and pour into a salad bowl or deep plate lined with lettuce leaves. Scatter the anchovies and herbs on top. *Serves 4–5.*

GREEK SALAD PLATTER

6 cooked medium potatoes diced
2 onions chopped
½ cup thinly sliced scallions (green onions)
¼ cup minced parsley
½ cup French dressing
Lettuce leaves, preferably iceberg
1 bunch watercress, stems removed
2 tomatoes sliced in thin wedges

2 small cucumbers cut in finger pieces
1 small avocado sliced
¾ cup blue cheese coarsely grated
1 small green pepper cut in rings
2 small cooked beets sliced or julienned
Greek olives
French dressing
2 tablespoons minced fresh orégano

1. Combine the potatoes, onions, scallions, and parsley with the ½ cup French dressing.

2. Line a large platter with the big outside leaves of the head of lettuce and pile the potato salad mixture in the center.

3. Tear up the rest of the head of lettuce and scatter it around the platter outside the potato salad.

4. Sprinkle the cress over the whole platter.

5. Arrange the tomato wedges around the outside of the platter, with cucumber fingers between.

6. Lay the avocado slices inside the tomato ring.

7. Scatter the cheese over the entire platter and lay the green pepper rings on top.

8. Next to the potato salad, on the inside, arrange beet slices or little bundles of julienned beets.

9. Scatter the olives all over.

10. Drizzle the platter with French dressing and scatter orégano over. *Serves 8–10.*

SCANDINAVIAN VEGETABLE SALAD

1 cup cooked green peas
1 cup cooked carrots diced
½ cup diced cooked beets
½ cup celery sliced thin
1 tablespoon minced fresh dill or
   1 teaspoon dried

1 tablespoon wine vinegar,
   preferably garlic flavored
Salt and pepper
4-6 tablespoons dairy sour cream
Chopped parsley
Sliced radishes, unpeeled

1. Toss together the peas, carrots, beets, celery, dill, vinegar, and salt and pepper to taste. Chill several hours.
2. At serving time blend the sour cream into the salad, arrange in a bowl, and garnish the top with parsley and radishes. *Serves 6.*

SPINACH SALAD

1 pound fresh spinach
1 bunch watercress
1 crushed garlic clove
½ teaspoon salt
½ teaspoon grated lemon rind
¼ teaspoon paprika
¼ teaspoon fresh-ground pepper

2 tablespoons vinegar, preferably
   tarragon
½ cup olive or salad oil
2 tablespoons dairy sour cream
6 slices bacon cooked crisp and
   crumbled

1. Wash and dry both spinach and watercress. Remove the large stems from both and the large veins from the spinach. Tear the spinach into bite-size pieces. Chill both.
2. Combine the remaining ingredients, except bacon, for the dressing. Beat the garlic, salt, lemon rind, paprika, pepper, and vinegar with a fork and gradually beat in the oil and sour cream.
3. Pour the dressing over the chilled greens, toss well, and scatter the crumbled bacon over the top. *Serves 4–6.*

SUMMER GARDEN SALAD

1 medium tomato cut in thin
  wedges
½ medium head cauliflower broken
  into flowerets
1 cup julienned cooked beets
  (canned will do)
1 cup cooked peas

1 cup sliced radishes, unpeeled
1 cup green beans, cooked and cut
  in 1-inch pieces
1 small head iceberg lettuce torn up
1 bunch watercress, washed,
  stemmed, and dried
French dressing

Toss all the ingredients lightly with just enough French dressing to moisten them. *Serves 6.*

WATERCRESS SALAD

REMOVE the large stems from 2 bunches of watercress. Wash and dry well. Put in a bowl, salt lightly, and cover. At serving time mix the juice of ½ lemon and 3 tablespoons olive oil. Pour over the cress and toss lightly. *Serves 4.*

ZUCCHINI-CAULIFLOWER SALAD

1 small head cauliflower, broken
  into flowerets and cooked just
  until tender
4 small zucchini, cut in diagonal
  ¼-inch slices and cooked 5 minutes

½ teaspoon salt
Italian-style dressing
Chopped parsley

1. The vegetables for this salad should be cooked with great care. They should be barely tender and still crisp. Drain them thoroughly. Cool.
2. Toss the vegetables lightly with just enough dressing to moisten and salt to taste. Pile on a plate of crisp lettuce and garnish lavishly with parsley. *Serves 6.*

ZUCCHINI-ENDIVE SALAD

6 small heads Belgian endive cut
   in 1-inch pieces
4 small zucchini thinly sliced
   diagonally

Salt and pepper
French or Italian dressing

BOTH vegetables can be raw for this salad, or the zucchini can be
cooked just 2 or 3 minutes in boiling salted water—not long enough
to soften it. Toss the vegetables lightly with dressing just to moisten.
Serves 4–5.

POTATO, PASTA, AND CEREAL SALADS

POTATO SALAD DUMAS

6 potatoes, peeled and cooked in
   chicken stock to cover
   Salt and pepper to taste
2 tablespoons salad or olive oil

2 teaspoons wine vinegar
2 cups dry white wine
2 tablespoons chopped parsley,
   chives, and chervil

1. Drain the potatoes well and slice thin.
2. Sprinkle the potatoes with salt and pepper, olive oil, vinegar, and
wine. Mix well and chill at least 2 hours.
3. Just before serving toss again lightly with chopped herbs. *Serves
6–8.*

SOUR CREAM POTATO SALAD

4 cups diced fresh-cooked potatoes
½ cup diced cucumber
1 tablespoon minced onion or shallots
¾ teaspoon whole celery seed
3 hard-cooked eggs

1½ teaspoons salt
½ teaspoon fresh-ground pepper
1½ cups dairy sour cream
½ cup mayonnaise
¼ cup vinegar
1 teaspoon prepared mustard

1. Toss together lightly the potatoes, cucumber, onion, celery seed, chopped whites of the hard-cooked eggs, and salt and pepper.
2. Mash the yolks of the eggs and blend with the sour cream, mayonnaise, vinegar, and mustard.
3. Stir the dressing into the potatoes and toss gently to blend. Allow to stand at least 15 minutes before serving. Garnish with crisp greens. *Serves 8.*

FRENCH-CANADIAN POTATO SALAD

8 medium potatoes peeled and boiled until just tender
3 teaspoons chopped parsley
Juice of 1 grated onion
2 tablespoons salad or olive oil

Salt and pepper
1 tablespoon vinegar
½ cup chicken or beef consommé

THIS potato salad is quite different from the conventional, and truly delicious.
1. Slice the hot potatoes into a bowl and immediately stir in the parsley, onion juice, oil, and seasoning to taste.
2. Mix the vinegar and consommé, pour over the potatoes, mix gently, and let cool gradually, at room temperature. Stir occasionally.
3. Chill only about 1 hour before serving. *Serves 8–10.*

LOUIS DIAT'S POTATO SALAD

5-6 potatoes, unpeeled, cooked
    until just tender
    Salt and pepper
2 tablespoons vinegar
6 tablespoons olive or salad oil
4 tablespoons warm water

2-3 scallions chopped (green
    onions)
1 tablespoon mixed parsley,
    chives, chervil, and tarragon,
    chopped (fresh)

1. Drain, peel, and slice the potatoes thin. Salt and pepper to taste at once.
2. Put the vinegar, oil, and water in a jar and shake well. Pour over the potatoes and toss gently.
3. Add the scallions and herbs and toss lightly again. Cool but do not chill. *Serves 6.*

HOT POTATO SALAD

8 medium potatoes cooked in their
    jackets until barely tender
¼ cup diced bacon
¼ cup chopped onion
2 teaspoons flour
2 teaspoons salt (scant)

Pepper to taste
⅓ cup vinegar
⅓ cup water
½ teaspoon celery seed
2 tablespoons chopped parsley

Hot potato salad (really just warm) is an old-time favorite, but still well liked by many people. It is of German origin.
1. Peel the hot potatoes and slice thin.
2. Cook the bacon until crisp. Skim out, crumble over the potatoes, and add the onion to the bacon fat.
3. Cook the onion lightly, until it just begins to color, and then blend in the flour, salt, and pepper. Stir in the vinegar mixed with the water, the celery seed, and the parsley. Pour over the potatoes and toss lightly. Serve at once, while still warm. *Serves 6–8.*

FRENCH POTATO SALAD

4-5 medium potatoes, cooked in
   their skins until just tender
1 teaspoon salt
Pepper to taste
⅓ tablespoons vinegar
⅓-½ cup salad oil

¼ cup white wine or water
1 tablespoon minced onion
Chopped fresh chives,
   parsley, chervil, or tarragon,
   or any mixture

1. Drain, peel, and slice the potatoes.
2. Mix salt, pepper, vinegar (use the smaller amount if you use wine, the larger if you use water), oil, wine or water, onion, and herbs. Shake well and pour over potatoes. Toss gently with fork and spoon to coat potatoes well with dressing. Serve warm or at room temperature—do not chill. *Serves 4.*

FRENCH POTATO AND BEAN SALAD

1 cup cooked string beans cut up
2 medium potatoes boiled, peeled,
   and diced
French dressing

3 small tomatoes sliced
6 black olives sliced
4 anchovy fillets cut in strips

THIS is similar to Niçoise salad, but has additional ingredients, such as tomatoes, olives, and anchovies, that give it a more exotic flavor.
1. Toss the beans and potatoes separately with French dressing, and let them marinate several hours in the refrigerator.
2. On a lettuce-lined platter arrange a circle of tomato slices around the outside edge.
3. Spread the beans inside the tomatoes and overlapping them, and the potatoes in the center, overlapping the beans.
4. Sprinkle the olives and anchovies over the potatoes, and serve with more French dressing. *Serves 4.*

RED POTATO SALAD

2 cups hot potatoes diced small
¾ cup dairy sour cream
1 tablespoon vinegar
Salt and pepper

1 cup cooked beets diced small
2 hard-cooked eggs chopped
coarsely
3 strips crisp bacon

1. Mix the sour cream with the vinegar, salt, and pepper.
2. Combine the sour cream mixture with the remaining ingredients. adding the crumbled bacon at the last minute. Serve slightly warm. *Serves 5–6.*

MACARONI SALAD

1½ cups elbow macaroni cooked
1½ cups chopped celery
½ cup minced onion
6 radishes thinly sliced
(unpeeled)
2 tablespoons minced parsley

¾ cup diced sharp Cheddar
cheese
1 large green pepper diced
1 cup mayonnaise
½ teaspoon dry mustard
1½ teaspoon salt
⅛ teaspoon pepper

1. Blend the macaroni gently but thoroughly with the celery, onion, radishes, parsley, cheese, and green pepper.
2. Stir into the mayonnaise the mustard, salt, and pepper, and combine this dressing with the macaroni mixture. Chill well. Before serving garnish with grated cheese or chopped parsley. *Serves 6.*

MACARONI AND VEGETABLE SALAD

3 cups cooked elbow macaroni
1 cup cooked green peas
½ cup cooked carrot diced
1 cup chopped celery
1 tablespoon chopped onion or
shallots

1 tablespoon Worcestershire or
A-1 sauce
1 cup mayonnaise
1 teaspoon salt
½ teaspoon paprika
Crisp lettuce leaves

1. Arrange the lettuce leaves to cover a deep plate or line a bowl.
2. Mix the remaining ingredients, correct seasoning, and pile onto lettuce. *Serves 6.*

114

TABBOULEE (Tomato-Mint Salad)

1 cup cracked wheat (bulgur)
1½ cups chopped parsley
¼ cup chopped fresh mint
½ cup chopped scallions (green onions) or minced onion

1 cup chopped ripe tomatoes, peeled
Salt and pepper
½ cup salad oil
¼ cup lemon juice

Bulgur is widely available in this country as wheat pilaf.
1. Soak the bulgur 2 hours in water to cover. Drain well.
2. Mix the bulgur with the parsley, mint, scallions, and tomato, and season to taste.
3. Shake up the oil and lemon juice together and pour over the bulgur. Toss lightly to blend well and correct seasoning. *Serves 4.*

FRUIT SALADS

CALYPSO FRUIT SALAD

7 medium size ripe bananas
1 cup dairy sour cream
¼ cup light rum
2 tablespoons brown sugar
¼ teaspoon ground ginger
⅛ teaspoon salt
2 teaspoons lime juice
Lettuce leaves

17-ounce can peach halves, drained and chilled
2 pint boxes strawberries or 2 packages frozen whole strawberries thawed and drained

1. Mash 1 banana with a fork and blend in the sour cream, rum, sugar, ginger, salt, and lime juice. Refrigerate at least 1 hour.
2. At serving time arrange a bed of lettuce on a large serving platter.
3. Slice the remaining bananas lengthwise and lay on the lettuce. Arrange the peach halves and strawberries on top, and cover with the chilled dressing. *Serves 6.*

FRUIT SALAD WITH POPPY SEED DRESSING

1 grapefruit cut in sections and
sections skinned
2 oranges sectioned and skinned
2 small avocados peeled and
sliced
¼ cup lemon juice
Watercress, washed and
stemmed
2 heads Belgian endive separated
into spears

Poppy Seed Dressing
½ cup sugar
1 teaspoon salt
1 teaspoon dry mustard
⅓ cup wine vinegar
2 teaspoons onion juice
1 cup salad oil
1½ tablespoons poppy seeds

1. Put the slices of avocado into the lemon juice to keep the color fresh.
2. Arrange watercress on serving plates, and the grapefruit and orange sections and avocado slices on top.
3. Pour the poppy seed dressing over the fruit and tuck the spears of endive in and around, leaving the ends out so they can be eaten with the fingers.
4. *The dressing:* Dissolve the sugar, salt, and mustard in the vinegar. Stir in the onion juice and oil. Add the poppy seeds and shake well. *Serves 4.*

FRUIT SALAD WITH MELON

Cantaloupe or honeydew melon
Diced pineapple
Fresh strawberries or raspberries

Seedless grapes
French dressing
Dairy sour cream or cottage cheese

1. Split the melon, remove the seeds, peel, and cut in bite-sized pieces.
2. Mix the melon with the other fruits in any proportion desired.
3. Blend the fruits with French dressing made with lemon juice and sweetened with a little sugar.
4. Serve on lettuce leaves and top each serving with a tablespoon of cottage cheese or sour cream.

116

FRUIT SALAD PLATTER I

ARRANGE a bed of shredded salad greens on a large platter. Place a mound of cottage cheese in the center of the platter and around it arrange groups of fruits: pineapple chunks, grapefruit sections, orange slices, apple slices, seedless or seeded grapes, melon balls, fresh plums halved and pitted, strawberries, raspberries, etc. Pass a sweet French dressing with the salad (*see Index*).

FRUIT SALAD PLATTER II

½ honeydew melon
½ cantaloupe
½ pineapple cut into cubes
2 oranges sectioned and skinned
2 grapefruit sectioned and skinned
1 red apple cut into thin slices
   (unpeeled)
   Strawberries, raspberries, or
   blueberries
1 tablespoon lemon juice
   Lettuce

Cream Mayonnaise
   ½ cup heavy cream whipped stiff
   2 tablespoons crumbled
     Roquefort cheese
1½ cups mayonnaise

Sour Cream Dressing

1 cup dairy sour cream
1 tablespoon lemon juice
   Salt to taste

1. Prepare the fruit and chill it well. Cut the melons into balls or into ¾-inch cubes, and brush the apple slices with lemon juice to prevent darkening.
2. Cover a large chilled platter with crisp lettuce leaves and lay the fruit in rows on the lettuce.
3. Scatter the berries all over the surface.
4. Serve with cream mayonnaise or sour cream dressing.
5. To make the dressings, blend ingredients well and chill. *Serves 6.*

FRUIT SALAD PLATTER III

ON a bed of watercress on a large platter place a good-sized ball of cream cheese rolled in chopped nuts. Arrange fruits around it in piles: strawberries or raspberries, seedless grapes or pitted Bing cherries, pineapple wedges, orange and grapefruit sections skinned, halved peaches with blueberries in the cavities, halved plums, and melon balls or wedges. Have a bowl of sweet French dressing or cream mayonnaise or both to accompany the salad (*see Index*).

TOSSED FRUIT SALAD

4 plums skinned and cut in 8 wedges each	1 pint fresh strawberries hulled or whole strawberries frozen and partly thawed
4 peaches skinned and cut in 8 wedges each or frozen sliced peaches thawed and drained	6 small clusters seedless green grapes
1 banana fluted and cut in ½-inch diagonal slices	⅓ cup lemon juice
	3 cups torn-up mixed greens
	½ cup watercress, stems removed

1. Prepare the fruits and sprinkle with lemon juice to keep the color. Flute the banana by drawing the tines of a sharp fork lengthwise along its surface. Chill well. (Save out a few berries to garnish the bowl or platter.)
2. Mix the fruit and torn-up greens, and toss gently with the dressing. Arrange in a large bowl or platter, and garnish with watercress, whole berries, and grape clusters.

Dressing

⅓ cup salad oil	2 tablespoons sugar
2 tablespoons wine vinegar	½ teaspoon salt
3 tablespoons lime juice	⅛ teaspoon paprika
¼ cup orange juice	3 tablespoons chopped fresh mint

MIX and chill the ingredients listed above. *Serves 4.*

118

STUFFED CANTALOUPE SALAD

4 cantaloupes halved and seeded
2 slices fresh pineapple diced
24 watermelon balls
12 grapefruit segments skinned
24 orange sections skinned

2 cups ripe raspberries
1 cup seedless grapes
French dressing
1 pint lime or lemon ice

1. Prepare and chill all the fruit.
2. Arrange the fruit in the cantaloupe halves, reserving a few raspberries for garnishing. Pour a little dressing over the fruit and chill ½ hour.
3. At serving time place a small scoop of fruit ice on top of each salad and top with a raspberry or a tiny sprig of mint. *Serves 8.*

Note: You can make smaller salads by cutting the cantaloupes into quarters instead of halves, and piling the fruit on. In this case the quantities given would make 16 servings.

FROZEN FRUIT SALAD

1 egg slightly beaten
¼ cup sugar
½ teaspoon salt
1½ tablespoons flour
¾ cup syrup drained from
    pineapple and pears
2 tablespoons vinegar

1 cup heavy cream whipped
3 bananas mashed
1 cup canned pears drained and
    diced
1 cup drained pineapple tidbits
12 maraschino cherries sliced

1. Combine the egg, sugar, salt, flour, syrup, and vinegar in a saucepan and cook over low heat until thick, stirring constantly. Chill.
2. When cold stir in the whipped cream and all the fruit. Blend carefully and pour into refrigerator trays. Freeze until solid, with the coldest setting of the refrigerator.
3. Cut in blocks and serve on lettuce leaves. *Serves 10–12.*

MOLDED SALADS

QUICK ASPIC

2 cups chicken stock
1 cup tomato juice
4 envelopes plain gelatin
  Salt and pepper

1 teaspoon sugar
2 eggshells crushed
2 egg whites, lightly beaten
2 tablespoons cognac

1. Combine all ingredients except the cognac in a saucepan and heat slowly, stirring constantly until the mixture boils up in the pan. Season to taste.
2. Strain through a sieve lined with a cloth wrung out in cold water.
3. Add cognac and chill until set. *Makes about 4 cups.*

AVOCADO MOUSSE

1½ tablespoons plain gelatin
  ½ cup cold water
  ½ cup boiling water
2½ cups mashed avocados (4-5
    medium)
  3 tablespoons chopped parsley

1 tablespoon lemon juice
½ teaspoon onion juice
1 teaspoon Worcestershire sauce
1 teaspoon salt
½ cup mayonnaise
½ cup heavy cream whipped

1. Sprinkle gelatin on cold water, dissolve in boiling water. Cool.
2. Mash the avocados with a silver fork and blend in the parsley, lemon and onion juices, Worcestershire sauce, and salt to taste.
3. Fold the mayonnaise and gelatin into the whipped cream and combine with the avocado mixture.
4. Pour into a quart mold rinsed in cold water and chill until firm.
5. Unmold on a chilled platter and garnish with stemmed sprigs of watercress and tomato quarters. *Serves 6.*

Serve with a chicken casserole (see Index) and buttered green peas.

120

AVOCADO-HAM MOUSSE

1 avocado peeled and seeded
¾ cup ground cooked ham
1 egg separated
10½-ounce can chicken broth

1 envelope plain gelatin
1 tablespoon lemon juice
½ cup heavy cream whipped

1. Add the slightly beaten egg yolk to ⅔ cup of the chicken broth and cook over low heat until somewhat thickened, stirring.
2. Sprinkle the gelatin on the cold chicken broth, add to the hot broth, and stir until the gelatin is dissolved. Chill until it begins to set.
3. Cut the avocado in pieces and put it into the blender with the lemon juice and blend until smooth. Or mash the avocado or push it through a sieve. In either case, add the lemon juice.
4. Blend the mashed avocado, the ham, and the gelatin. Fold in the egg white beaten until stiff and the whipped cream. Pour into a 9-inch ring mold and chill until firm.
5. Unmold on a chilled platter and garnish with radish roses and ripe olives, and also with slices of another avocado. Serve with mayonnaise. *Serves 8.*

Serve with frozen spinach soufflé thawed and arranged in a ring mold to bake, and hot bread or rolls.

AVOCADO, FIG, AND GRAPEFRUIT SALAD MOLD

1 package lemon-flavored gelatin
2 cups water
1 avocado, peeled and sliced
1 grapefruit separated into sections
  and skinned

1 cup canned figs drained
Mayonnaise

1. Dissolve the gelatin in water according to package instructions.
2. In the bottom of a lightly oiled ring mold arrange a pattern of avocado slices and grapefruit sections. Pour in some of the gelatin mixture and chill until set. Arrange the rest of the avocado slices and grapefruit sections with the figs to fill up the mold and add the remaining gelatin. Chill until firm.
3. Unmold the salad on a serving plate, surround with crisp torn-up lettuce, and serve with mayonnaise. *Serves 6.*

MOLDED AVOCADO AND TUNA

Avocado Layer
1 large avocado peeled and
  mashed
1 envelope plain gelatin
¾ cup water
2 tablespoons lemon juice
½ cup dairy sour cream
½ cup mayonnaise
1 teaspoon salt
Dash Tabasco sauce

Tuna Layer
6½ or 7-ounce can tuna rinsed and
  coarsely flaked
1 envelope plain gelatin
1¼ cup water
3 tablespoons lemon juice
1 teaspoon salt
1 cup diced celery
⅓ cup diced pimiento

1. Make the avocado layer first. Sprinkle gelatin on water to soften and stir over low heat to dissolve. Chill to raw-egg-white consistency.
2. Blend the remaining ingredients into the gelatin and pour into a 9" x 5" loaf pan. Chill until almost firm.
3. For the tuna layer, dissolve the gelatin in ½ cup of the water over low heat. Remove from heat and stir in the rest of the water, lemon juice, and salt. Chill to the consistency of raw egg white.
4. Fold in the remaining ingredients and chill until it begins to set.
5. Pour the partially set tuna gelatin on top of the avocado layer and chill until firm.
6. Unmold on a chilled platter and garnish with torn-up salad greens, stuffed olives, spears of celery, and tomato wedges. *Serves 8.*

Serve with peas orégano and cucumbers in sour cream (see Index).

BLENDER AVOCADO RING MOLD SALAD

1 evelope plain gelatin
½ cup cold water
1 medium avocado peeled and
  diced
1 tablespoon lemon juice
1 cup dairy sour cream

1 teaspoon sugar
¼ teaspoon salt
½ teaspoon onion salt
Dash cayenne
½ cup mayonnaise

122

THIS is an exceptionally easy and delicious salad for a hot day.

1. Sprinkle the gelatin over the cold water and dissolve over hot, stirring until dissolved.

2. Put this gelatin and all the other ingredients into a blender, cover, and blend about 1 minute. Scrape down with a rubber scraper if necessary.

3. Pour the avocado mixture into an oiled ring mold. Cover with foil and chill until firm.

4. Unmold the salad on a serving platter and fill the center with one of the main-course salads in a preceding section: crabmeat, lobster, tuna, or chicken. *Serves 6.*

GUACAMOLE MOLD

3 envelopes plain gelatin
1 cup cold water
2 medium tomatoes peeled and quartered
2 one-pound ripe avocados cut in pieces
2 tablespoons lemon juice

¼ cup green pepper cut up
½ cup onion cut up
1 teaspoon seasoned salt
⅛ teaspoon fresh-ground pepper
1 scant teaspoon chili powder
1 cup dairy sour cream
1 cup mayonnaise

THIS salad has the smooth velvety quality of all avocado salads, but the flavor is heightened with a number of other ingredients.

1. Sprinkle the gelatin on 1 cup of cold water and let stand 5 minutes. Stir over low heat until gelatin is dissolved. Refrigerate until it is the consistency of unbeaten egg white.

2. Put in a blender the tomatoes, avocados, lemon juice, green pepper, onion, salt, pepper, chili powder, sour cream, and mayonnaise. Blend 1 minute.

3. Add the partly set gelatin to the avocado mixture and blend again ½ minute. Pour into an oiled 1½-quart melon mold and chill at least 4 hours, or overnight.

4. Unmold on a chilled platter and garnish with tomato wedges and sprigs of parsley. *Serves 6–8.*

JELLIED BEET AND HORSERADISH SALAD

2 tablespoons plain gelatin
2 tablespoons cold water
2 cups boiling water
½ cup lemon juice
½ cup sugar
1½ tablespoons prepared
  horseradish

1 tablespoon vinegar
½ teaspoon salt
Few drops Worcestershire sauce
¾ cup finely chopped cabbage
¾ cup shredded cooked beets

1. Sprinkle the gelatin over the cold water and dissolve in the boiling water.
2. Combine the gelatin with the lemon juice, sugar, horseradish, vinegar, salt, and Worcestershire sauce. Chill until it begins to set.
3. Stir the cabbage and beets into the partially set gelatin and pour into a mold. Chill until firm.
4. Unmold on a bed of crisp greens and serve with mayonnaise. *Serves 5–6.*

CHEESE RING WITH VEGETABLE SALAD

½ cup bleu cheese softened
2 three-ounce packages cream
  cheese softened
¼ cup milk
2 teaspoons Worcestershire sauce
¼ teaspoon paprika
1 tablespoon gelatin
¼ cup water

1 cup cream whipped
3 cups torn-up salad greens
1 cucumber peeled and diced
⅔ cup sliced radishes, unpeeled
⅔ cup grated carrots
⅔ cup minced green pepper
Salt
French Dressing

1. Soften the cheeses until they can be combined well. Stir in the milk, Worcestershire sauce, and paprika.
2. Sprinkle the gelatin over the water and dissolve over hot water. Stir in the cheese mixture and blend well. Fold in the whipped cream and turn into a 1-quart ring mold rinsed in cold water. Chill until firm.
3. Mix all of the vegetables, season to taste, and toss with enough French dressing to coat them evenly.
4. Unmold the cheese ring on a platter and pile the vegetable salad in the center. Serve at once, while the vegetables are still crisp. *Serves 6–8.*

MOLDED CHICKEN AND PINEAPPLE SALAD

1½ cups diced cooked or canned chicken
½ cup canned crushed pinapple drained well
1 envelope plain gelatin
1½ cups chicken stock

½ teaspoon salt
¼ cup pineapple syrup drained from fruit
2 tablespoons lemon juice
½ cup diced celery

1. Sprinkle the gelatin on half the chicken stock and dissolve over low heat, stirring constantly. Remove from heat and add the rest of the stock, salt, pineapple syrup, and lemon juice. Chill to raw-egg-white consistency.
2. Fold in the chicken, pineapple, and celery, turn into a small mold rinsed in cold water, and chill until firm.
3. Unmold on a chilled plate and garnish with salad greens. Serve with mayonnaise. *Serves 4.*

Serve with jellied beet and horseradish salad, asparagus with sour cream (see Index), and hot rolls of some kind.

CUCUMBER AND GRAPEFRUIT MOLD

1-pound can grapefruit sections
1 envelope plain gelatin
1 tablespoon sugar
¼ teaspoon salt

1 tablespoon vinegar
Few drops green vegetable coloring
1 cup diced peeled cucumber

1. Drain the syrup from the grapefruit sections and add enough water to make 1¾ cups liquid.
2. Mix this liquid with the gelatin, sugar, and salt, and stir over low heat until the gelatin is dissolved.
3. Stir in the vinegar and a little green food coloring. Chill to the consistency of unbeaten egg whites.
4. Fold in the cucumber and grapefruit, pour into a ring mold rinsed out in cold water, and chill until firm. Unmold on a chilled platter and serve with mayonnaise. *Serves 6.*

CUCUMBER AND PINEAPPLE MOLD

2 envelopes plain gelatin
¼ cup cold water
3½ cups canned pineapple juice
    heated
¼ cup lemon juice

¼ cup tarragon vinegar
Few drops green food coloring
2 cups chopped peeled cucumber
1 cup crushed pineapple drained
½ teaspoon salt

THIS pretty and flavorful salad is a favorite with many people.

1. Sprinkle the gelatin on the cold water and dissolve in the hot pineapple juice. Cool and add the lemon juice and vinegar. Stir in a little green food coloring. Chill until syrupy.

2. Fold in the pineapple and cucumber and pour into a ring mold which has been rinsed in cold water. Chill until set.

3. Unmold on a chilled platter and fill the center with torn-up mixed salad greens which have been well tossed with French dressing. Pass mayonnaise too. *Serves 6–8.*

DEVILED EGG SALAD MOLD

1 envelope plain gelatin
2 tablespoons cold water
1¾ cups chicken broth
3 hard-cooked eggs
1 tablespoon dairy sour cream or
    mayonnaise

½ teaspoon vinegar or lemon juice
½ teaspoon prepared mustard
Salt and pepper
1 teaspoon fresh basil, chervil, and
    marjoram mixed or ½ teaspoon
    dried

1. Soften the gelatin in the cold water. Add a little chicken broth to it and heat until dissolved, stirring constantly. Add to the rest of the chicken broth and chill until the consistency of unbeaten egg white.

2. Devil the eggs. Cut in half lengthwise and remove the yolks to a small bowl. Mash the yolks and add the sour cream or mayonnaise, vinegar or lemon juice, mustard, seasoning to taste, and herbs. Fill the whites with this mixture.

3. Place the stuffed egg halves, stuffed side down, in the bottom of a small mold. Pour the partially set gelatin around and over them and chill until set. Serve with mayonnaise mixed with additional herbs and sour cream. *Serves 4–5.*

MOLDED FRUIT SALAD

1 package lemon-flavored gelatin
1 cup hot water
½ cup cold water
1 ripe banana cut in half
  lengthwise and crosswise

12 Bing cherries, pitted and halved
2 peaches, peeled and quartered
12 melon balls 1-inch in diameter

1. Stir the gelatin into the hot water until dissolved. Add cold water.
2. Pour ½ cup of the gelatin mixture into a chilled oiled quart mold and refrigerate. Put the rest of the gelatin in the refrigerator to be cooled to syrup consistency.
3. When the gelatin in the mold has set, place the fruit on it in an attractive layer. Cover with more gelatin and chill until almost set. Repeat layers until ingredients are used up, and chill until firm.
4. Unmold onto a bed of torn-up lettuce or stemmed watercress. Serve with mayonnaise. *Serves 6.*

GINGER ALE FRUIT SALAD

1 envelope plain gelatin
2 tablespoons cold water
½ cup boiling water
1 tablespoon sugar
  Dash salt
1 cup ginger ale
2 tablespoons lemon juice
½ cup heavy cream whipped
½ cup sliced and seeded or
  seedless white grapes

1 cup pineapple tidbits well
  drained
½ cup chopped nuts

Fruited Cream Dressing
⅓ cup mayonnaise
⅓ cup dairy sour cream
2 tablespoons pineapple juice

1. Soften the gelatin in cold water and dissolve in boiling water. Stir in the sugar, salt, ginger ale, and lemon juice. Chill until the consistency of unbeaten egg whites.
2. Fold in the whipped cream, grapes, pineapple, and nuts. Chill until firm.
3. Unmold and serve on lettuce leaves with fruited cream dressing, made by blending the ingredients until smooth. *Serves 6.*

GOLDEN SALAD

1 envelope plain gelatin
¼ cup sugar
¼ teaspoon salt
¾ cup pineapple juice, canned,
  fresh, or frozen
¼ cup orange juice
¼ cup vinegar

1 cup diced canned pineapple well
  drained
½ cup orange sections cut up and
  drained
½ cup coarsely grated raw carrots
⅓ cup chopped nuts (optional)

1. Mix the gelatin, sugar, and salt in a small saucepan. Add the pine-apple juice. (If you use fresh or frozen juice, not canned, boil 2 minutes before measuring.) Put the saucepan over low heat and stir constantly until the gelatin is dissolved. Remove and stir in the orange juice and vinegar. Chill to the consistency of raw egg white.

2. Fold in the pineapple, oranges, carrots, and nuts, and pour into a mold rinsed out with cold water. Chill until firm.

3. Unmold on a chilled platter and surround with torn-up salad greens. Serve with mayonnaise. *Serves 6.*

GRAPEFRUIT RING MOLD

4 envelopes plain gelatin
½ cup cold water
2 cups hot water
½ cup sugar
1½-2 cups syrup from the grapefruit

½ cup lemon juice
Few drops green food coloring
2 one-pound cans grapefruit
  sections

1. Sprinkle gelatin over cold water and dissolve in hot water over low heat. Add sugar, syrup, lemon juice, and a bit of green food coloring. Chill until the consistency of unbeaten egg whites.

2. Arrange half of the grapefruit sections in a ring mold and cover with some of the partially set gelatin. Chill until firm.

3. Arrange the rest of the grapefruit sections on the partly set ring and cover with the remaining gelatin. Chill until firm.

4. Unmold on a chilled platter, surround with torn-up salad greens tossed with a little French dressing, and serve with mayonnaise. *Serves 6–8.*

MOLDED GRAPEFRUIT-AVOCADO SALAD

2 twenty-ounce cans grapefruit sections
Canned grapefruit juice
2 envelopes unflavored gelatin

⅓ cup sugar
½ teaspoon salt
1½ cups diced avocado
½ cup diced celery
Pimiento

1. Drain the grapefruit sections and add enough grapefruit juice to the syrup to make 3½ cups.
2. Put 1 cup of the grapefruit juice in a small saucepan, sprinkle the gelatin on it, and heat over low heat until the gelatin is dissolved, stirring constantly.
3. Add the sugar and salt to the hot juice and stir into the rest of the juice. Chill until the consistency of raw egg whites.
4. Fold in the well-drained grapefruit sections, the avocado, and the celery. Pour into a mold rinsed out in cold water, and chill until set. *Serves 8–10.*

GRAPEFRUIT-GINGER SALAD

1 envelope plain gelatin
2 tablespoons sugar
⅛ teaspoon salt
1-pound can unsweetened grapefruit sections

2 tablespoons lemon juice
¼ cup chopped celery
¼ cup diced tart apples
1 teaspoon chopped crystallized ginger

1. Mix the gelatin, sugar, and salt in a small saucepan.
2. Drain the syrup from the grapefruit and add enough water to make 1¼ cups of liquid. Add ½ cup of this liquid to the gelatin saucepan and dissolve over low heat, stirring constantly. Remove from the heat and add the rest of the syrup and the lemon juice. Chill to the consistency of unbeaten egg white.
3. Fold into the gelatin mixture the well-drained grapefruit, celery, apples, and ginger. Pour into a 3-cup mold and chill until firm.
4. Unmold the salad on a serving dish and garnish with torn-up salad greens and avocado slices. *Serves 6.*

JELLIED LIME-MELON SALAD

1 envelope plain gelatin
3 tablespoons cold water
1 cup hot water
½ cup lime juice

½ cup sugar
¼ teaspoon salt
1½ cups melon balls (or 1 package frozen thawed)

1. Soften gelatin in cold water and dissolve in hot water. Stir in lime juice, sugar, and salt. Chill until the consistency of raw egg whites.
2. Fold in the melon balls and chill until set.
3. Unmold on a chilled plate, garnish with salad greens, and serve with mayonnaise. *Serves 4.*

PEACH-CHEESE RING

¼ pound bleu cheese softened
1 pint cottage cheese
1 teaspoon Worcestershire sauce
Few drops Tabasco sauce
1 envelope plain gelatin

¼ cup cold water
½ cup mayonnaise
½ cup heavy cream whipped
#2½ can peach halves drained

1. Cream the cheeses together until well blended. Work in the Worcestershire sauce and Tabasco.
2. Soften the gelatin in the cold water and dissolve it over hot water, stirring constantly.
3. Mix the mayonnaise and whipped cream and fold into the dissolved gelatin.
4. Arrange the peach halves, smooth side down, in the bottom of a ring mold.
5. Blend the mayonnaise-cream mixture with the cheese mixture and pour over the peaches in the mold. Chill until set.
6. Unmold on a chilled platter and garnish with torn-up lettuce. *Serves 8.*

JELLIED PEAR SALAD

1½ ounces cream cheese
  (½ small package)
4 stuffed olives minced
6 pear halves
6 strips pimiento

1 tablespoon gelatin
¼ cup cold water
1 cup boiling water
½ cup lemon juice

1. Mash the cheese until soft and blend in the chopped olives. Stuff the pear cavities with this mixture. Lay strips of pimiento across the pears and place, cut side down, in individual molds.
2. Sprinkle the gelatin over the cold water and add the boiling water, stirring until the gelatin is completely dissolved. Stir in the lemon juice. Chill until it barely begins to set.
3. Pour the gelatin over the pears until the molds are full and chill until firm.
4. Unmold the salads on crisp lettuce and serve with mayonnaise. *Serves 6.*

PINEAPPLE NUT MOLDED SALAD

2 packages lime gelatin
1 cup hot water (boiling)
#2 can crushed pineapple,
  undrained

1 pint dairy sour cream
½ cup chopped nuts
½ cup chopped maraschino
  cherries

1. Dissolve the gelatin in the boiling water, stirring until dissolved.
2. Stir in the pineapple with its juice, and chill until the consistency of unbeaten egg whites.
3. To the chilled gelatin mixture add the sour cream, nuts, and cherries. Stir well and pour into a ring mold that has been lightly oiled. Chill until set.
4. Unmold on a large chilled platter and garnish with fresh fruit and destemmed sprigs of watercress. Serve with mayonnaise. *Serves 6.*

TOMATO-EGG MOLD

2 cans prepared tomato aspic or
  Quick Tomato Aspic (see Index)
2 tablespoons plain gelatin
½ cup water
3-ounce package cream cheese
1 cup mayonnaise
1 tablespoon cider vinegar

1-2 teaspoons prepared horseradish
3 hard-cooked eggs coarsely
  chopped
½ cup chopped celery
2 tablespoons chopped onion
¼ cup chopped green pepper

1. Melt the canned aspic and pour into a loaf pan rinsed in cold water. Chill until almost set.
2. Sprinkle the gelatin over the water and dissolve over hot water, stirring.
3. Beat together the cream cheese, mayonnaise, vinegar, and horse-radish.
4. Fold in the eggs and vegetables and stir in the dissolved gelatin.
5. Pour this mixture on top of the chilled aspic and chill until set.
6. Unmold the loaf on a chilled platter and serve with mayonnaise.
Serves 6–8.

TUNA MADRILÈNE SALAD

Seven-ounce can tuna, drained
  and coarsely flaked
1 envelope plain gelatin
¼ cup cold water
2 twelve-and-a-half ounce cans
  madrilène consommé

1 cup chopped cucumber
Salt
2 tablespoons chopped onion
½ cup mayonnaise
1 tablespoon prepared horseradish

1. Soften gelatin in the cold water. Heat 1 can of the madrilène to boiling and stir in the gelatin. Continue stirring until gelatin is dis-

solved. Add second can of madrilène and chill until the consistency of raw egg white.

2. Combine carefully the tuna, cucumber, salt to taste, and onion, and add to madrilène. Chill.

3. Stir the horseradish into the mayonnaise and combine with the chilled salad. Refrigerate until firm.

4. Unmold on a chilled platter and garnish with torn-up crisp greens and tomato wedges. *Serves 6–8.*

Serve with hot buttered mixed vegetables and potato chips.

TUNA SOUFFLÉ SALAD

2 seven-ounce cans tuna, drained and coarsely flaked	½ cup mayonnaise
	¼ teaspoon salt
1 package lemon-flavored gelatin	Dash of pepper
1 cup hot water	1 cup minced celery
½ cup cold water	4 tablespoons minced parsley
3 tablespoons vinegar	1½ tablespoons minced onion

1. Dissolve gelatin in hot water and add the cold water, vinegar, mayonnaise, salt and pepper. Mix well and pour into refrigerator tray. Chill in freezing unit 15–20 minutes, until firm around the edges but still soft in the center.

2. Combine the tuna with the celery, parsley, and onion. Blend well.

3. Pour the slightly frozen gelatin mixture into a bowl and whip with a rotary beater or mixer until fluffy.

4. Fold in the tuna mixture, correct seasoning, and chill about 1 hour (not in the freezing compartment).

5. Unmold the salad on a chilled platter and surround with torn-up salad greens lightly tossed with French dressing. *Serves 6–8.*

Serve with mixed vegetable salad (see Index), sliced tomatoes, and hot rolls.

 # VEGETABLES

This section is concerned primarily with summer vegetables, and especially with those likely to be grown in the family garden. Some attention is given to frozen vegetables also, since they are so convenient and so time-saving.

VEGETABLE GHIVETCHI

1½ cups young carrots sliced thin
2 potatoes diced
½ medium eggplant peeled and diced
1 can tiny white onions drained
½ cup each peas, lima beans, and green beans (frozen will do)
½ green pepper cut in strips
½ small cabbage sliced fine
1 small cauliflower cut up
½ summer squash diced

½ celery root diced (optional)
5 small tomatoes quartered
3 cloves garlic mashed
2 small onions sliced thin
¼ cup butter or margarine or salad oil
1 cup consommé or chicken broth
½ cup olive oil
1 tablespoon salt
Fresh-ground pepper

THIS is a good dish for a party buffet, and can be completely prepared in the morning, leaving only the baking to dinnertime.
1. Arrange all of the vegetables except the sliced raw onions in a large casserole in layers, preferably in the order in which they are listed.
2. Sauté the sliced onions in butter until golden.
3. Add to the onions the consommé or chicken broth, olive oil, salt and pepper, and bring just to a boil.
4. Pour over the casserole, cover tightly, and bake 30–40 minutes in a moderate oven, 350°, until the vegetables are tender. Stir once or twice while baking. *Serves 12–14.*

Serve with baked ham, tossed green salad, and hot buttered rolls.

VEGETABLE MELEE

¼ pound butter or margarine
1 cup cut green beans
1 cup celery cut in diagonal slices
1 cup frozen peas or lima beans,
  thawed

2 cups scraped and sliced carrots
2 cups peeled and diced potatoes
1 head iceberg lettuce cut in small
  cubes
Salt and pepper
1 cup thin-sliced onions

THIS is a good dish for a large gathering, and, like the preceding one, can be completely prepared in the morning, except for baking.
1. Melt a little of the butter in the bottom of a large, heavy casserole, and arrange the vegetables, layer by layer, except for the onions, dotting each with bits of butter and salt and pepper.
2. In what butter remains lightly sauté the onions and spread over the top.
3. Cover the casserole tightly (with foil if necessary) and bake 1 hour in a moderate oven, 350°. Stir the contents after 20 minutes, and again 20 minutes later. The vegetables should be reasonably tender, but still crisp. *Serves 12–15.*

Serve with a roast chicken, a tossed green salad, and hot garlic bread.

QUICK VEGETABLE CASSEROLE

2 packages lima beans partly
  cooked
2 packages cut corn thawed or
  fresh corn cut off the cob
16-17-ounce can tomatoes

4-ounce can whole mushrooms
1 teaspoon onion salt
½ teaspoon celery salt
1 teaspoon sugar
3 tablespoons butter or margarine

MIX the vegetables in a large casserole, with the onion and celery salt and sugar. Dot with the butter. Cover and bake 25–30 minutes in a moderate oven, 375°. *Serves 6.*

ASPARAGUS-CHEESE SOUFFLÉ

1 cup shredded American cheese
1 can condensed cream of asparagus soup

6 eggs separated
Salt and pepper to taste

1. Add the cheese to the soup and heat, stirring constantly, until the cheese is melted.
2. Stir in the slightly beaten egg yolks and cool to lukewarm.
3. Beat the egg whites until stiff but not dry and fold into the soup-cheese mixture. Season to taste.
4. Pour the mixture carefully into an ungreased medium casserole and bake in a slow oven, 300°, 1–1¼ hours, or until the soufflé is golden brown and a knife inserted in the middle comes out clean. Serve at once. *Serves 6.*

Serve with a platter of cold cuts or cold fried chicken, a vegetable salad (see Index), and hot rolls.

RATATOUILLE

Olive or salad oil
3 large onions chopped fine
3 large green peppers seeded and
diced
6 small zucchini, unpeeled, cut in
¼-inch slices
1 medium eggplant, unpeeled,
diced

6 large tomatoes peeled, seeded,
and diced
1 cup chopped parsley
3 cloves garlic minced
Salt and pepper
Grated Parmesan cheese

1. Cover the bottom of a large heavy skillet with oil and lightly sauté the onions, until they begin to show a little color. Add the green peppers and cook a couple of minutes more. Add the zucchini and eggplant and cook 5 minutes, or until they begin to look transparent.
2. Pour all these vegetables into a large casserole, and stir in the tomatoes. Cover and either simmer over very low heat for 1½ hours or bake in a slow oven, 300°, for 2 hours. Stir in the parsley and garlic, season to taste, and cook another 20 minutes.
3. Sprinkle with plenty of grated Parmesan cheese. Serve either hot or well chilled. *Serves 8.*

PAN-BRAISED VEGETABLES

VEGETABLES pan-braised without water are much more flavorful than those boiled in water, and are certainly easy to do.

Place 2 tablespoons of butter or margarine in a heavy skillet that has a tight-fitting lid (or make a lid out of heavy-duty foil). Add the vegetables, salt them, add a bit of sugar, a little chopped onion or garlic if you like, and cover the vegetables with a layer of the outside leaves of lettuce or romaine. Cover tightly, bring to a quick boil, and turn the heat to low. Various vegetables require about the following times to cook tender:

asparagus, 15 minutes
cut green beans, 15 minutes
thin sliced beets, 15–18 minutes
cut-up broccoli, 15 minutes
thin-sliced cabbage, 10 minutes
sliced or diced carrots, 15 minutes
cauliflower flowerets, 15 minutes

corn cut off the cob, 5–10 minutes
green peas, 15 minutes
cut-up fresh spinach, 3 minutes
summer squash cut up or sliced, 10 minutes
sliced zucchini, 10 minutes

ASPARAGUS WITH SOUR CREAM

2½-pound bunch fresh asparagus
1 cup dairy sour cream
Salt and pepper
2 tablespoons lemon juice
2-3 tablespoons butter or margarine
½ cup fresh bread crumbs

1. Cook the asparagus until barely tender and drain. Arrange in a shallow baking dish.
2. Mix the sour cream with salt and pepper to taste and stir in the lemon juice. Spread over the asparagus.
3. Melt the butter in a small pan and stir the crumbs in it. Sprinkle the buttered crumbs on top of the sour cream. Bake in a hot oven, 400°, 3–4 minutes. *Serves 6–8.*

QUICK GREEN BEAN CASSEROLE

2 packages French-style green
beans
1 package French-fried onion rings
thawed

2 cans cream of mushroom soup
½ cup top milk or thin cream

1. Cook beans in boiling salted water, not over 3 minutes after they come to a boil. Drain well.
2. Alternate layers of beans and onions in a medium casserole, ending with onions on top.
3. Stir the milk into the soup and pour over the casserole. Bake 25 minutes in a 350° oven. *Serves 6.*

GREEN BEANS ALMONDINE

2 packages frozen cut or French-
style green beans or 1 pound
fresh, cut in 1-inch diagonals
½ cup butter or margarine
1 teaspoon salt

¼ teaspoon sugar
Few lettuce leaves
½ cup blanched slivered almonds
2 tablespoons lemon juice
Dash pepper

1. Melt half of the butter in a good-sized skillet and add the beans, salt, and sugar. Stir well and cover with a layer of lettuce leaves. Cover tightly, bring to a quick boil, turn the heat very low, and cook about 10 minutes, or until just tender. Or cook the beans in a minimum amount of salted water until tender but still crisp. Drain.
2. Sizzle the remaining butter (or all of it if the beans are cooked in water), and brown the almonds quickly, stirring constantly. Add the lemon juice, a grind of fresh pepper, and pour over the beans. *Serves 6–8.*

138

GREEN BEANS NIÇOISE

¼ cup salad oil
1 medium onion or 6 scallions
(green onions) sliced thin
2 tomatoes peeled and quartered
½ green pepper diced small
1 stalk celery chopped

Salt and pepper
¼ cup water
Bouquet garni
1 pound green beans cut in 1-inch
diagonals and partly cooked

1. Heat the oil and in it cook the onion, tomatoes, green pepper, celery, salt and pepper to taste. Add the water and the bouquet garni (2 cloves, 1 small bay leaf, 6 sprigs parsley, and ½ teaspoon chervil tied in cheesecloth) and cook until the vegetables are tender and the sauce reduced a little—about 15 minutes.
2. Stir in the beans and finish cooking them, which should not take more than 5 minutes. (Cook them 5 minutes or less the first time.) *Serves 4.*

ITALIAN GREEN BEANS WITH WATER CHESTNUTS

¼ cup butter or margarine
1 cup (a 5-ounce can) water
chestnuts, drained and sliced

2 packages frozen Italian green
beans
½ cup consommé

THIS is a pleasant combination, and takes only a few minutes to prepare.
1. Melt the butter in a heavy skillet, add the water chestnuts, and sauté them lightly for a few minutes, stirring constantly.
2. Stir in the beans, mixing well, and keep stirring until the beans are well broken up.
3. Add the consommé, bring to a boil, cover tightly, turn the heat low, and simmer about 5 minutes, or until the beans are tender but still crisp. *Serves 6.*

BROCCOLI OR ASPARAGUS CASSEROLE

2 ten-ounce packages frozen
broccoli or asparagus
1 cup grated Cheddar cheese
1 can cream of mushroom soup

⅔ cup evaporated milk (1 small
can)
3½-ounce can French-fried onion
rings

1. Cook the frozen vegetable only 4 minutes in boiling salted water. Drain and arrange in shallow casserole. Sprinkle the cheese over it.
2. Mix the soup with the evaporated milk and pour over. Bake in a moderate oven, 350°, 25 minutes.
3. Remove the casserole from the oven, spread the onion rings over the top, and return to the oven for 8–10 minutes longer. *Serves 6–8.*

LEMON CARROTS

2 pounds carrots scraped and cut
in ½-inch dice
½ cup melted butter or margarine
2 tablespoon sugar

2 teaspoons minced parsley
1 teaspoon paprika
Juice 1 lemon

THIS is a simple way to "dress up" carrots a bit, with next to no trouble, to appeal to people who don't like them.
1. Simmer the carrots in salted water until tender. Drain.
2. Add to the pan the remaining ingredients, stir well, and cook 5 minutes, shaking the pan 2 or 3 times to coat the carrots well with the sauce. *Serves 5–6.*

CUCUMBERS IN SOUR CREAM

SLICE 1 large cucumber and 1 large onion very thin. Rub the bowl you will use with a cut clove of garlic. Place the onion on the bottom, the cucumber on top. Make a dressing of ¾ cup dairy sour cream, 2 tablespoons vinegar, 1 teaspoon salt, 1 teaspoon sugar, a grind of pepper, and ¼ teaspoon dry mustard. Mix well and pour over the cucumbers, cover, and chill at least an hour. *Serves 4–5.*

140

PEAS OREGANO

¼ cup butter or margarine
1 package frozen green peas
½ teaspoon salt
1 tablespoon lemon juice

1 tablespoon instant minced onion
½ teaspoon dried orégano or
1½ teaspoons fresh, chopped

MELT the butter in a saucepan which has a tight cover. Add all the
other ingredients, stir gently, cover, and cook 10–15 minutes over
medium heat. *Serves 3–4.*

ANCHOVY POTATOES

12 medium potatoes cut in
julienne strips
4 medium onions sliced
20-24 anchovy fillets cut up

4 tablespoons butter or
margarine
2-2¼ cups heavy cream

1. In a greased casserole make alternate layers of potatoes, onions,
anchovies, and butter, ending with a layer of potatoes. You will
probably not need salt with the anchovies.
2. Bake 10 minutes in a 400° oven. Pour over half the cream and
bake 20 minutes more.
3. Add the rest of the cream, reduce the heat to 300°, and continue
baking another 20 minutes, or until tender. *Serves 8–10.*

BAKED NEW POTATOES

SCRUB potatoes well with a vegetable brush, but do not peel them.
Place about 1 pound in the center of an 18-inch square of heavy-
duty foil. Add 1 tablespoon butter or margarine, 2 tablespoons water,
and 1 teaspoon salt. Seal the packet well with double seams and bake
1 hour in a 325° oven. Add more melted butter before serving. *One
pound serves 3–4.*

SLICED POTATOES BAKED IN FOIL

THIS is an exceptionally delicious way to fix potatoes, and an easy one, that can be prepared hours before dinnertime, except for baking.

Peel potatoes and cut in ¼-inch slices. Put the slices in the center of a piece of heavy-duty foil well oiled, piling the potatoes on top of one another. Sprinkle each slice of potato with 1 scant teaspoon onion soup mix and a little butter—no salt. Seal the packet with double seams and bake in a 375° oven or on an outdoor grill over hot coals 45 minutes, or until tender. Open the packet and dish up the potatoes. (Three medium potatoes will serve 4 people.)

GRUYÈRE POTATOES

Garlic
Butter or margarine
2 pounds potatoes peeled and
  sliced thin
1 cup milk scalded with 2-3 onion
  slices

1 egg beaten
Grated nutmeg
Salt and pepper
Grated Gruyère cheese

1. Rub a good-sized casserole with a cut clove of garlic and butter it well. Arrange the sliced potatoes in it.
2. Strain the onion out of the milk, and blend the milk with the egg, a good pinch of nutmeg, salt and pepper to taste, and pour over the potatoes.
3. Sprinkle the potatoes thickly with cheese, dot with butter, and bake 40–45 minutes in a moderate oven, 350°. *Serves 6–8.*

QUICK SCALLOPED POTATOES

1 can condensed cream of
  mushroom soup
½ cup milk
Salt and pepper to taste

1 tablespoon minced onion
5 cups cooked potatoes sliced
2 tablespoons butter or margarine

142

1. Heat the soup and stir in the milk, salt and pepper, and onion.
2. In a greased medium casserole make alternate layers of potatoes and soup. Dot each layer with a little butter.
3. At the end pour any leftover soup over the casserole and use any remaining butter to dot the top.
4. Cover and bake 30 minutes in a 375° oven. Remove the cover for the last 15 minutes. *Serves 6.*

BAKED SLICED IDAHOS

PEEL medium Idaho potatoes and slice, holding each one firmly so that it more or less keeps its shape as you slice. As you finish a potato lift it to a shallow buttered casserole and press so that the slices spread out, leaning on one another with a little overlap. Sprinkle the casserole with salt and grated cheese, half Parmesan and half Swiss. Drizzle over quite a lot of melted butter or margarine and bake 20 minutes in a very hot oven, 500°, or 30 minutes in a 400° oven. To serve, lift the potato slices out with a spatula. *Two good-sized Idahos serve 3 people.*

GREEN SUCCOTASH

Corn cut from 8 ears	2 tablespoons butter
¾ pound or 1 package French-style green beans cooked just 2 minutes	1 teaspoon salt
	½ teaspoon sugar
	¼ teaspoon pepper
1½ cups light cream (scant)	Few drops Tabasco sauce

COMBINE all the ingredients in a saucepan and simmer about 10 minutes. *Serves 4–5.*

TIAN

½ pound dried white beans soaked overnight in water to cover
Salt and pepper to taste
6 tablespoons salad oil
7-9 small zucchini, unpeeled, diced small
1½ garlic cloves mashed
2 pounds spinach or 2 packages frozen
2 teaspoons fresh orégano chopped or ¾ teaspoon dried
½ cup grated Parmesan cheese
½ cup bread or corn-flake crumbs
5 anchovy fillets minced

THIS is a delicious casserole, outstanding for a party dish, especially for a buffet.
1. Drain the soaked beans, cover with a quart of fresh water, and simmer, covered, until the beans are so tender that the skin will break if you blow on one in a spoon. Just before they are done, salt to taste. Drain, stir in 2 tablespoons oil, and stir well.
2. Cook the zucchini in the remaining 4 tablespoons oil, adding the garlic to the oil. Cook the zucchini about 6 minutes, stirring frequently, or until tender. Skim the zucchini slices out into a large casserole.
3. Cook the spinach in the oil remaining in the zucchini skillet, drain, and press out all the water you can.
4. Make layers of the ingredients on top of the zucchini: 2 layers of beans, 2 layers of spinach. Season each layer with salt and pepper and orégano.
5. Top the casserole with a mixture of the cheese, crumbs, and anchovies and bake in a 350° oven about 45 minutes, or until the topping is golden and the cheese melted. *Serves 10.*

BAKED SUMMER SQUASH

PEEL 3–4 young summer squash, slice thin, and arrange in layers in a casserole which has a tight cover (or make a lid of foil). Salt and pepper each layer, dot with butter or margarine, sprinkle lightly with flour. At the end add 3–4 tablespoons milk. Cover the casserole tightly and bake 1 hour at 350°. *Serves 3–4, depending upon size of squash.*

144

ZUCCHINI PIERETTE

1 pound small zucchini, unpeeled,
   cut in ¼-inch slices
2 tablespoons Cointreau
3 tablespoons flour
1 ½ tablespoons butter, margarine,
   or salad oil

1 teaspoon salad oil
4 teaspoons fresh tarragon
   chopped or 1½ teaspoons
   dried

1. Sprinkle the sliced zucchini with the Cointreau and stir in the flour.
2. Heat the 1½ tablespoons butter or margarine, and oil, in a heavy skillet and sauté the zucchini slices until they are a delicate brown.
3. Sprinkle with tarragon just before serving. *Serves 4.*

ZUCCHINI WITH ARTICHOKE HEARTS

4 small zucchini, unpeeled, cut in
   ¼-inch slices
9-ounce package frozen artichoke
   hearts

8-ounce bottle Italian-style salad
   dressing
1 large tomato cut in thin wedges
Salt and pepper
Chopped parsley

1. Put the zucchini in a saucepan with the artichoke hearts and dressing. Bring to a boil and simmer, covered, about 10 minutes, or until tender. Drain, but reserve the liquid. Chill well, at least 4 hours.
2. When ready to serve arrange on a platter and arrange tomato wedges on top. Pour the reserved liquid over, season lightly, and sprinkle generously with parsley. *Serves 6.*

✣ OUTDOOR COOKING

All over America the back-yard grill has become almost as common a sight as the television aerial, and al fresco eating is part of the summer routine. Recipes play a small part in this kind of cooking, and this section, therefore, is chiefly devoted to a timetable for grilling over charcoal. A few suggestions for picnic menus are also given.

GRILLING OVER CHARCOAL

BACK-YARD grills come in so many sizes and styles, from the small Japanese hibachi to the lordly grill that will take steaks or chops or hamburgers for a crowd, that probably the best thing a cookbook can do in this field is to offer a few general guides and suggest times for grilling various foods.

The most important general caution for broiling meats over charcoal is to be sure the fire is right. A charcoal fire should be started early enough so that it is burned down to the point where all the charcoal is covered with gray ash. This ash should be knocked off by stirring it a bit before food is put on the grill.

If you are grilling lean meat or fish, rub the grill first with a piece of fat or with cooking oil to keep the food from sticking. In many cases it is best to put the food in a hand grill which can be laid on the big grill.

To avoid flame-ups while meat is grilling, keep the fire moderate or increase the distance of the grill from the heat. If flame-ups still occur, as they well may, have a bottle of water handy with a sprinkler top, or squirt water on the hottest part with a long Pyrex baster.

Lean meats should be basted frequently while grilling.

146

TIMETABLE FOR GRILLING OVER CHARCOAL

TIME for grilling is hard to specify, since it depends upon several factors: the heat of the fire, the thickness of the food to be grilled, its distance from the heat, and the degree of doneness desired. For example, here are average times for grilling a sirloin or porterhouse steak, taking these factors into consideration, all 3 inches from the heat. These times are *total* grilling times. Steaks should be turned at the halfway point. The best temperature for grilling steak is a medium one, 350° to 375°, which can be measured by an oven thermometer placed flat on the grill. The grill should be thoroughly preheated before starting to grill a steak.

Thickness	Rare	Medium	Well Done
1 inch	7–12 minutes	12–15 minutes	15–20 minutes
1½ inches	10–14 minutes	15–18 minutes	18–25 minutes
2 inches	18–25 minutes	25–35 minutes	35–60 minutes
2½ inches	30–35 minutes	35–45 minutes	45–75 minutes

T-BONE STEAKS 1½ inches thick take about 9–13 minutes on each side for medium rare.

CLUB STEAKS 1½ inches thick take 6–10 minutes per side.

SCORED FLANK STEAKS ¾ inch thick take 5–6 minutes per side, 2 inches from heat.

MARINATED ROUND STEAK 1 inch thick takes 12 minutes per side 3 inches from heat.

HAMBURGERS ½ inch thick need 15 minutes total time, to be turned once.

SPARERIBS take long slow grilling, starting with low heat, and with frequent basting. A total time of 1 hour is needed.

PORK CHOPS 1 inch thick need 30–40 minutes, 3 inches from heat, turned once.

RIB OR LION LAMB CHOPS, 1–2 inches thick, need 12 minutes per side, 3 inches from heat.

CHICKEN HALVES OR PIECES, 1½–2½-pound chickens, need a total time of 25–35 minutes, 2–3 inches from heat. Baste often with a mixture of ⅓ cup vinegar, ⅓ cup lemon juice, ⅓ cup salad oil, ½ teaspoon soy sauce, and salt and pepper, shaken up in a jar.

DUCKLING (3–5 pounds, ¼ duckling per person) needs 45–60 minutes, 3 inches from the heat. Wash and dry well before grilling and turn often.

FISH STEAKS (salmon, halibut, haddock, swordfish) should be about 1 inch thick. Broil 3 inches from heat about 12 minutes, turning once. Fish is easier to grill in a hand grill, well greased, which makes them easy to turn.

LOBSTER, 1–1½ pound. Have them split and cleaned and lay them on the grill shell side down, 3 inches from heat. Brush often with melted butter. Grill 15 minutes, turn, and grill 5 minutes longer. A total of 20 minutes is needed.

LOBSTER TAILS, one ½-pound tail per serving. Slit the underside with scissors or a very sharp knife, the full length of the tail. Brush the slit side with melted butter and put shell side down on the grill, 3 inches from the heat. Grill for 15 minutes, brush with more melted butter, turn, and grill 3 minutes more—a total of 18 minutes.

HAM STEAK. Lay a steak 1½–2 inches thick in a hand grill to facilitate turning. Grill 15 minutes per side. Pineapple slices can be laid on one side of the steak if desired.

SHISH KEBAB (see Index). On the outdoor grill broil it 15 minutes close to the heat, turning once.

Serve with a big bowl of potato salad, a bubbling casserole of macaroni and cheese brought out from the kitchen, a large platter of spaghetti with cheese or tomato sauce or both, a pot of Boston baked beans, or a similar main dish, and corn on the cob cooked on the grill (see Index), as well as a large green salad, sliced tomatoes, and hot buttered rolls.

PICNIC MENUS

THE menu for a picnic will depend partly on whether or not you will be able to have a fire at your picnic place or on the beach, in which case usually hamburgers or frankfurters are the main item of the meal. But most real picnics nowadays are not built around a fire, and the only hot dish will be one you bring from home. It is quite possible to take a good hot casserole with you, even a considerable distance, if you take the hot casserole out of the oven just as you leave and wrap it well in many thicknesses of newspaper. Baked beans are a good choice, for example. Many of the casseroles in the section on Main Course Dishes can be carried in this way. And many of the cold salads can be carried in a gallon thermos jug or a cooler.

Cold meat pies are wonderful fare for a picnic on a hot day. Among those included in this book try Scottish Meat Pie, Cold Veal and Ham Pie, or Cold Chicken Pie (see Index). Baked Ham for a Crowd is another good item to take on an elaborate picnic (see Index). Deviled eggs, for which several recipes are included here, are especially good on a picnic, provided they are well chilled when made and carried along in a thermos or cooler.

Salad is always welcome on a picnic. If you want a tossed green salad carry the crisped greens in a plastic bag in a cooler and shake them up when ready with French dressing carried in a well-capped jar. (Don't forget forks and paper plates.) Or make a batch of cole slaw and carry it in a cooler or a large thermos. Provide sliced tomatoes too.

Fruit and cookies serve admirably as a dessert, especially if the cookies are brownies. And coffee can be carried in a big thermos if it cannot be made at the picnic place.

BACKYARD BARBECUED CHICKEN

3-pound chicken cut up for frying ½ cup soy sauce
  or quartered 1 teaspoon powdered ginger
1 cup dry white wine 1 clove garlic crushed

1. Put the wine, soy sauce, ginger, and garlic in a jar and shake up well.
2. Put the chicken pieces in a glass bowl, pour the marinade over, and chill several hours.
3. At serving time drain the chicken pieces on paper towels, and grill over a good charcoal fire, turning several times and basting with the marinade. *Serves 4.*

Serve with a quick vegetable casserole (baked in the house) and a large mixed vegetable salad (see Index).

GRILLED HAM STEAKS

THIS is a good dish for the back-yard grill.
1. Grill ¾-inch steaks of smoked ham 15 minutes over charcoal, turning frequently.
2. When they are almost done, brush both sides of the steaks with a mixture of 2 teaspoons dry mustard and 4 tablespoons honey. Turn the steaks 2 or 3 times to get a good glaze, cooking them about 5 minutes longer.

Serve with a cold vegetable salad (see Index) and a platter of sliced tomatoes, each slice topped with a dab of French dressing mixed well with chopped fresh herbs.

FOIL-ROASTED CORN

HUSK the corn and brush the ears with soft butter or margarine. Sprinkle each ear with a little salt and pepper and wrap in a piece of heavy-duty foil large enough to make a double seam down the side and turn in the top and bottom. Place the corn on a grill over a hot fire or over charcoal and cook about 15 minutes, turning several times.

ROASTED CORN

THIS is an alternate way to roast corn on an outdoor grill, and probably a little easier, though not as easy to manage for eating.

Pull the husks *back,* not off, and remove all the silk from each ear. Replace the husks. Soak the ears 10 minutes or so in a bucket of water (at the beach sea water serves beautifully for this). Shake off the water and lay the ears on a grill, over hot coals but not *on* them, and let them steam about 20 minutes if the corn is young, 25 minutes if on the mature side. Turn occasionally.

 # DESSERTS

For those who must have a dessert if a meal is to be considered complete, summer is the prime time for fruit desserts, and hence this section has more fruit desserts than any other kind. Frozen and molded desserts also have their place, however, and there are a few pies.

FRUIT DESSERTS

PLAIN FRUIT DESSERTS

1. *Oranges, grapefruit,* and *tangerines.* Peel, remove all membranes, keep segments whole.
2. *Pears and apples.* Peel or not, as you choose. Cut in cubes or wedges, dribble with lemon juice, or soak in orange or grapefruit juice.
3. *Melon, cantaloupe or honeydew.* See Index.
4. *Pineapple.* Slice and cut in thin wedges.
5. *Banana.* Brush with lemon or orange juice.
Mix fruit and chill well. Add a little sugar if necessary. Drain before serving, add 2–3 tablespoons brandy or kirsch if desired and let stand ½ hour.

FRESH FRUIT AND CHEESE FOR DESSERT

1. Fresh pears and Gorgonzola cheese
2. Walnuts, raisins, and Cheddar, Muenster, or hickory-smoked cheese

3. Halved, cored, and peeled pears mounded with cream cheese blended with apricot jam
4. Thin slices of unpeeled red apples dipped in lemon juice to preserve their color, with slices of Cheddar or bleu cheese
5. Berries or plums with Petit Suisse cheeses
6. A variety of fruits arranged on a tray with a variety of cheeses— Brie, Muenster, Gouda, bleu, Camembert, etc.

QUICK CANNED-FRUIT DESSERTS FOR SUMMER

1. PEARS SEVILLE. Drain pear halves. Cover with melted orange marmalade and top with sour cream.
2. PEACH CRUNCH. Sprinkle drained canned peach halves with ½ tablespoon brown sugar, 1 tablespoon corn-flake crumbs, cinnamon, and dots of butter (per half). Bake 15 minutes at 375°. Serve warm with cream or ice cream.
3. QUICK CHERRIES JUBILEE. Drain a 17-ounce can of pitted black Bing cherries. To ¼ cup of the syrup add 1 cup currant jelly and heat until melted. Add the cherries and heat. Stir in 2 tablespoons kirsch before pouring over ice cream. Or warm the kirsch, ignite, pour flaming over the cherries, and serve flaming at the table.

FROSTY FRUIT CUP

10-ounce package frozen
  raspberries
14-ounce can frozen pineapple
  chunks

½ cup port wine
1 pint mint, lemon, lime, or
  pineapple sherbet

PARTIALLY defrost the fruit. Spoon into serving dishes and top with scoops of sherbet. *Serves 4–5.*

GRAND MARNIER SAUCE FOR FRUITS

3 egg yolks
¼ cup sugar
1 cup milk scalded

2 cups heavy cream
½ cup confectioners' sugar
¼ cup Grand Marnier liqueur

1. Beat yolks and sugar together well, add milk gradually, and cook over low heat, continuing to beat, until the sauce thickens but does not boil. Cool.
2. Whip the cream with the confectioners' sugar until soft peaks form when the beater is lifted.
3. Stir the Grand Marnier into the cooled custard and blend in the whipped cream. Chill well.

Serve this sauce cold over heated fruits flavored with kirsch— peaches, rhubarb, applesauce, etc.

FRESH FRUIT WITH BAR-LE-DUC DRESSING

1 peach
1 banana
1 apricot
1 orange
1 nectarine
1 pear
Few seedless grapes
1-2 slices fresh pineapple
½ cup bar-le-duc dressing
2 tablespoons lime juice

Chilled cantaloupes
Fruit sherbet

Bar-le-Duc Dressing
1 cup olive or salad oil
¼ cup tarragon vinegar
1 teaspoon salt
½ teaspoon pepper
¼ teaspoon sugar
¼-½ cup bar-le-duc preserves

1. Peel, slice, and cut the fruit, except cantaloupes, into bite-sized pieces and place in a large bowl.
2. Mix the ingredients of the bar-le-duc dressing. Combine the lime juice with ½ cup dressing and sprinkle over fruit. Blend well.
3. Halve the cantaloupes, remove seeds, and fill with fruit. Top with a scoop of lime, lemon, or orange sherbet. Garnish with a strawberry, a few blueberries, and a sprig of fresh mint. *Serves 6. Allow ½ or ¼ cantaloupe per person.*

154

FRUIT SALAD DESSERT

2 fresh peaches sliced
4 maraschino cherries halved
2 tablespoons slivered crystallized
  ginger
1 large orange sectioned (remove
  membranes)

2 plums peeled and quartered
2 teaspoons confectioners' sugar
½ cup mayonnaise
½ cup dairy sour cream
¼ cup pistachio nuts

MIX the fruit gently together. Mix the sugar, mayonnaise, sour cream, and blend lightly with the fruit. Chill well and sprinkle with pistachio nuts before serving. *Serves 3–4.*

MACEDOINE OF CANNED FRUIT

USE 4–6 varieties of canned fruit, depending upon the number to be served. Drain all the syrups into a saucepan and boil hard for 10–15 minutes to reduce somewhat.

Put the fruits in a bowl. For each cup of fruit add 1 tablespoon of the reduced syrup and 1 tablespoon brandy. Cover and refrigerate at least 2 hours.

When ready to serve, arrange the fruits in a decorative bowl, spoon over a little more of the syrup, and sprinkle with ¼–½ cup chilled Curaçao or Grand Marnier liqueur. Garnish with fresh mint.

FRUIT MELANGE

1 cup fresh or canned peaches
  sliced
6 apricot halves, canned or fresh
6 slices fresh or canned pineapple

3 bananas cut in half lengthwise
  and crosswise
1 glass raspberry jelly
Blackberries or raspberries

ARRANGE peaches, apricots, and pineapple in sherbet glasses, and top each with one banana piece. Melt the jelly and pour over the fruit. Top with berries. *Serves 6.*

MACEDOINE OF FRUIT FLAMBÉ

4 tablespoons butter
2 pears peeled, cored, and sliced
½ cup pineapple diced
1 cup strawberries

1 banana sliced
1 cup apricot purée
½ cup warm rum

HEAT the butter in a large heavy skillet and lightly sauté the fruit, just until it is all well heated. Mix in the apricot purée and heat 1 minute longer. Pour the warm rum over and blaze. Serve over slices of pound cake. *Serves 4–5.*

COUPE MADELEINE

2 cups honeydew melon diced
1 tablespoon confectioners' sugar
Dash of salt
1 tablespoon fresh lime juice

1 pint vanilla ice cream
1 cup red currant jelly melted over
hot water
1 tablespoon lemon juice

THIS is a dessert that cannot be made ahead of time, except for preparing the melon. Just before serving, combine the melon, sugar, salt, and lime juice. Put a small helping in sherbet glasses. Cover the melon with a scoop of ice cream and pour over all the melted jelly which has been mixed with the lemon juice. *Serves 6.*

FLAMING PEACH-CHERRY DESSERT

THAW 1 box of frozen sliced peaches or cut up 2 cups of fresh peaches and mix them with one jar of cherry preserves. Warm 3 ounces of brandy, ignite, and pour flaming over the fruit. Serve flaming. *Serves 4.*

HAWAIIAN AMBROSIA

2 cups peeled orange sections
1 cup fresh pineapple cubes
1 cup shredded coconut
1 cup orange juice

2 teaspoons grated orange rind
1 teaspoon finely minced preserved
ginger

Mix and chill well. *Serves 6.*

BANANAS AND ORANGES WITH RUM

8 bananas peeled and slit
lengthwise
3 unpeeled oranges sliced thin
Brown sugar

½ cup butter or margarine
½ cup rum warmed

1. Arrange the bananas close together in a buttered shallow casserole and lay the orange slices over them, overlapping somewhat.
2. Cover the oranges with a thick layer of brown sugar, dot with butter, and bake in a slow oven, 300°, 30 minutes, or until bananas are soft.
3. Pour the rum over and ignite. Serve at once, with ice cream on top if desired. *Serves 8.*

BAKED BANANAS CARIBBEAN

6 medium bananas peeled and
scored with a fork
¼ cup lemon juice
13½-ounce can pineapple chunks
drained (save liquid)

2 tablespoons prepared mustard
¼ cup light brown sugar, firmly
packed
Dash cinnamon
⅛ teaspoon grated nutmeg

1. Lay the bananas in a lightly greased shallow casserole and brush them well with some of the lemon juice.
2. Put the pineapple juice in a small saucepan and add the remaining lemon juice, mustard, sugar, cinnamon, and nutmeg. Bring to a boil.
3. Arrange the pineapple chunks over the bananas, baste with the liquid, and bake in a medium oven, 375°, 30 minutes. Baste frequently. Serve warm or chilled. *Serves 6.*

BLACKBERRIES WITH COCONUT CREAM

8 ounces cream cheese softened
1 cup dairy sour cream
Confectioners' sugar

½ cup grated coconut
2 quarts chilled blackberries,
picked over

WHIP the cream cheese and sour cream together until fluffy. Sweeten to taste with sugar, blend in the coconut, and pour over the chilled blackberries without mixing. *Serves 6–8.*

BLUEBERRY BETTY

⅓ cup butter or margarine melted
2 cups very small bread cubes
4 cups fresh blueberries
½ cup brown sugar, packed
Pinch salt

2 tablespoons lemon juice
¼ cup bread or corn-flake crumbs
1 cup whipping cream or 1 pint
ice cream or hard sauce

1. Mix the butter well with the bread cubes and make a layer of the bread in a buttered casserole. Cover with a layer of blueberries.
2. Sprinkle the blueberry layer with half the brown sugar, salt, and lemon juice. Repeat layers until ingredients are used up.
3. Spread the crumbs in a thin layer for a topping, cover, and bake in a 350° oven about 40 minutes. Uncover the last 15 minutes to brown the crumbs. Serve with whipped cream, ice cream, or hard sauce. The dessert can be served either warm or chilled. *Serves 6.*

QUICK AND EASY BLUEBERRY PUDDING

NOTHING could be simpler than this blueberry dessert, and it is as good as it is simple.

Cut crusts from 6 thick slices of stale bread and spread them on

158

both sides with butter or margarine. Lay them in a shallow casserole or a pie plate, cutting them to fit the bottom tightly.

Put 4 cups of blueberries in a saucepan with ¾ cup of sugar and ¾ cup of water, and cook them until most of the berries are soft. Pour berries and juice carefully over the bread, cover, and chill several hours or overnight. Serve with a scoop of vanilla ice cream on each serving. *Serves 6–8.*

MELON BALLS IN WHITE WINE

PUT fresh or frozen, partly thawed, cantaloupe and honeydew melon balls in sherbet glasses and pour chilled dry white wine over.

CREAM AMBROSIA

1 cup heavy cream
½ cup dairy sour cream
3½-ounce can flaked coconut
1 cup miniature marshmallows

2 cups orange sections skinned
1½ cups grapefruit sections skinned
6 maraschino cherries (optional)

WHIP the cream stiff and fold in the sour cream, coconut, and marshmallows. Refrigerate several hours and then fold in the well-drained orange and grapefruit sections. Top each serving with a maraschino cherry if desired. *Serves 6.*

ORANGE, DATE, AND ALMOND MEDLEY

5 oranges peeled and sliced
1 cup dates coarsely diced
⅔ cup orange juice

2 tablespoons Grand Marnier liqueur (optional)
½ cup toasted slivered almonds

CUT the orange slices in half and mix them with the dates, orange juice, and Grand Marnier, if you use it. Chill at least 2 hours and stir in the nuts. *Serves 6.*

ORIENTAL ORANGES

8 navel oranges
16 pitted dates cut up
8 figs cut up
8 marshmallows cut up
2-3 tablespoons grated coconut
1 tablespoon honey or brown
  sugar

½ teaspoon ground cloves, nutmeg,
  and cinnamon mixed
Juice of ½ lemon
¾ cup blanched, slivered, toasted
  almonds
4 teaspoons Curacao liqueur
  (optional)

1. Slice off the top ½ or ¾ inch of the oranges and remove the flesh and membranes, keeping the skin intact. Drain the juice into a bowl while you operate on the oranges. Cut the orange meat into small pieces.
2. In a medium bowl mix the cut-up orange pieces, dates, figs, marshmallows, coconut, honey, spices, and lemon juice.
3. Put 1 tablespoon orange juice into each orange shell and fill the shells with the fruit mixture.
4. Arrange the stuffed oranges in a baking pan, sprinkle them with the almonds, and bake 30 minutes in a 350° oven.
5. Cool the oranges to lukewarm and pour ½ teaspoon of Curaçao over each one before serving. *Serves 8.*

PEACH CRUNCH

5 medium peaches peeled and
  cut up
1 teaspoon cinnamon (scant)
1 cup sugar
1 tablespoon butter or margarine

1 egg
½ cup sifted flour
½ teaspoon baking powder
Pinch of salt

1. Pile up the peaches in a 9- or 10-inch pie plate or shallow casserole; they will shrink in the baking. Sprinkle with cinnamon and ⅓ cup of the sugar.

160

2. Cream the butter and remaining sugar together and stir in the slightly beaten egg.

3. Sift the flour, baking powder, and salt together and stir into butter-sugar-egg mixture to make a smooth batter.

4. Push this batter in small tablespoons over the peaches, and don't worry if there are a few gaps.

5. Preheat the oven to 425°, but reduce the heat to 350° when you put in the peaches. Bake 20 minutes. Serve either warm or well chilled with cream or ice cream over it. *Serves 6.*

PEACH-PLUM COBBLER

2 cups fresh peaches peeled and quartered
2 cups fresh plums quartered
1 cup light brown sugar, firmly packed
2 tablespoons flour
2 tablespoons butter or margarine
Pastry for 1-crust pie

1. Arrange the peaches and plums in an 8″ x 8″ x 2″ pan. Mix the sugar and flour and sprinkle over. Dot with butter.

2. Place the pastry over the filling, folding the edge under just *inside* the pan. Cut slits near the center.

3. Bake 35 minutes in a hot oven, 425°. Serve warm with cream.

Note: For a different kind of top crust combine 1 cup packaged biscuit mix with 2 tablespoons sugar and ½ cup milk. Sprinkle a little sugar on top when it has been rolled or patted out. *Serves 5–6.*

QUICK AND EASY PEACH-RASPBERRY DESSERT

FOR each person to be served place 2 medium or 1 large peach half, fresh or canned, in a dessert dish. Fill the hollow with slivered almonds. Spoon over fresh or frozen raspberries. Top with sweetened cream or softened ice cream and more almonds.

CELESTIAL PEACHES

12 canned peach halves, or fresh   1 pint vanilla ice cream
  peaches, peeled   ¼ cup finely chopped walnuts
¼ cup ginger syrup   6 candied cherries

ARRANGE the peach halves cut side up in a shallow casserole or baking pan. Pour a little ginger syrup into each half and bake in a moderate oven, 350°, until lightly browned. Cool.

When ready to serve put 2 peach halves together with a scoop of ice cream. Garnish with chopped nuts and cherries. *Serves 6.*

PEACHES WITH RASPBERRY SAUCE

1 cup water   2 quarts fresh raspberries or
½ cup sugar   2 packages frozen, partly
1-inch piece vanilla bean   thawed
6 peaches peeled   ¼ cup kirsch (optional)
¾ cup apricot jam   ¼ cup toasted slivered almonds

1. Put the water, sugar, and vanilla bean in a saucepan and bring to a boil.
2. Add the peaches to the boiling syrup and poach 15–20 minutes, or until the peaches are tender.
3. Remove the vanilla bean and lift the peaches with a slotted spoon to a glass serving bowl.
4. Melt the jam in another saucepan, stir in the raspberries, and stir gently until well blended and the raspberries are somewhat cooked.
5. Stir the kirsch into the raspberry mixture and pour over the peaches. Top with the almonds. *Serves 6.*

COLD PEACH SOUFFLÉ

12-ounce package frozen sliced peaches, thawed, or 6 fresh peaches peeled and cut up
½ cup peach syrup
1 envelope plain gelatin
4 eggs separated

¼ cup water
1 tablespoon lemon juice
⅛ teaspoon salt
¼ teaspoon almond extract
½ cup sugar
1 cup heavy cream whipped

1. Drain the syrup from the thawed peaches and sprinkle the gelatin on it.
2. Beat the egg yolks and water together and add to the syrup. Cook in a double boiler over boiling water, stirring until the gelatin is dissolved, about 5 minutes.
3. Remove the top of the double boiler and stir in the lemon juice, salt, and almond extract. Chill 15 minutes.
4. Force the peaches through a coarse sieve or blend them 30–40 seconds, until smooth, and mix into the gelatin mixture.
5. Beat the egg whites until stiff but not dry and beat in the sugar. Fold both the egg whites and the whipped cream into the gelatin mixture. Turn into a 1½-quart soufflé dish and chill until firm. Or make a collar of folded foil or brown paper around the edge of a quart soufflé dish (straight-sided) and use that. Make the collar 4 inches wide and tie it around the edge of the dish so that it extends 2 inches above the dish. Garnish with more sliced peaches, preferably fresh. *Serves 6–8.*

POACHED PEARS

POACH large peeled and cored pear halves in a sugar syrup flavored with either a piece of vanilla bean or almond extract. When the pears are translucent, drain them, arrange each in a dessert dish, and stuff the cavities with maraschino cherries and almonds very finely chopped and mixed. Chill the pears. Boil down the syrup to half its volume and spoon a little over each pear half. Sugar syrup is made by boiling 2 cups sugar with 2 cups water 5 minutes.

CRISPY BAKED CANNED PEARS

ROLL drained pear halves in fine almond macaroon crumbs and arrange them in a shallow casserole or baking pan. Put 1 teaspoon brown sugar in the hollow of each pear. Mix ½ cup pear juice with ½ teaspoon nutmeg and pour over. Bake in a moderate oven, 375°, 25 minutes, or until lightly browned. Serve warm with cream or ice cream. *Serves 8.*

PINEAPPLE-CHERRY ANGEL

1 can frozen pineapple chunks
2 cups pitted black cherries (Bing), drained
½ cup port wine
1 cup heavy cream whipped

2 tablespoons sugar
1 tablespoon light rum
¼ cup diced currant jelly
Angel food cake

1. Cut both ends from the frozen pineapple can and push the pineapple into a dish. Pour the drained cherries over, and add the port. Cover and marinate several hours or overnight.
2. Combine the whipped cream, sugar, rum, and jelly.
3. Cut the angel food into individual serving pieces and arrange on dessert plates. Cover with pineapple-cherry mixture, carefully drained. Top with the whipped cream mixture. *Serves 6.*

PINEAPPLE WITH RUM SAUCE

DRAIN a can of fancy pineapple slices, saving the juice, and chill the fruit. Put the juice in a saucepan with ½ cup sugar and juice of ½ lemon, and boil until reduced a third. Cool and add 4 tablespoons light rum just before serving. Pour the syrup over the chilled pineapple slices and sprinkle with chopped cashew nuts and chopped preserved ginger.

164

PINEAPPLE MINT WHIP

2 egg whites beaten until stiff but
not dry
4 tablespoons confectioners' sugar
½ cup heavy cream whipped
2 tablespoons chopped fresh mint

½ teaspoon lemon juice
¾ cup drained fresh pineapple
chopped or canned crushed
pineapple

1. Add the sugar gradually while beating the egg whites. Fold in the whipped cream and the mint.
2. Stir the lemon juice into the pineapple and combine the mixtures. Chill well and garnish with a sprig of fresh mint when serving. *Serves 4.*

PINEAPPLE-ALMOND DESSERT SALAD

2 eggs beaten
3 tablespoons sugar
4 tablespoons vinegar
2 tablespoons pineapple juice
drained from can
1 teaspoon flour

Pinch of salt
#2½ can pineapple tidbits
(2½ cups)
1 cup slivered blanched
almonds
1 cup heavy cream whipped

1. Put in the top of a double boiler the eggs, sugar, vinegar, pineapple juice, flour, and salt and cook until thick, stirring frequently.
2. Remove from the heat and stir in the well-drained pineapple and almonds. Cover and chill several hours, or overnight.
3. Blend in the whipped cream and chill several more hours. *Serves 4-6.*

PINEAPPLE-STRAWBERRY DESSERT

1 ripe pineapple cubed
1 quart strawberries hulled

2 tablespoons sugar
¼ cup Cointreau liqueur (optional)

COMBINE the fruit with the sugar and gently stir in the Cointreau. Chill. Serve with sweetened whipped cream, dairy sour cream, or vanilla ice cream. *Serves 6.*

PINEAPPLE-COCONUT DELIGHT

1⅔ cups crushed pineapple
1 envelope plain gelatin
¼ teaspoon vanilla
½ cup instant nonfat dry milk

½ cup ice water
2 tablespoons lemon juice
¼ cup sugar
½ cup flaked or shredded coconut

1. Drain the pineapple well and add enough water to the juice to make 1 cup of liquid. Sprinkle the gelatin on the liquid and dissolve over low heat, stirring constantly.
2. Remove the juice from the heat and add the pineapple and vanilla. Chill to the consistency of unbeaten egg whites.
3. Mix the dry milk with the ice water and beat until soft peaks form —3–4 minutes. Add the lemon juice and continue beating until firm peaks form. Add the sugar gradually.
4. Fold the whipped milk into the gelatin mixture and stir in the coconut. Spoon into dessert glasses and chill well. *Serves 6–8.*

RASPBERRY TRIFLE

1 pint raspberries
Sugar to taste
6 eggs separated
½ cup sugar

1 cup dry white wine
Almond macaroons
Pinch salt
6 tablespoons sugar

1. Sugar the raspberries to taste and set aside.
2. Beat the egg yolks well and gradually stir in the ½ cup sugar and the wine. Put in the top of a double boiler and cook over boiling water, stirring constantly, until it is thick enough to coat a silver spoon. Cool.
3. Crumble enough macaroons to make a ½-inch layer on the bottom of an oven-proof glass serving bowl.
4. Cover the crumbs with alternate layers of berries and custard until both are used up.
5. Beat the egg whites until stiff but not dry, gradually stir in the 6 tablespoons sugar, and beat until well blended.
6. Spread the meringue over the trifle and bake in a slow oven, 300°, 15–20 minutes, or until a delicate brown. Chill until serving time. *Serves 6.*

STRAWBERRY-RASPBERRY-PISTACHIO MELBA

PUT in a saucepan a large jar of raspberry jelly (not jam) and 1 cup light corn syrup. Cook, stirring constantly, until the jelly is dissolved. Cool and stir in ¼ cup Cointreau liqueur. Pour the sauce over 2 cups of cleaned and hulled strawberries and chill. Use this as a topping for 1 quart of pistachio ice cream. *Serves 6.*

STRAWBERRY CREAM

MASH 1½ quarts cleaned and hulled strawberries and force them through a coarse sieve, or put them in a blender and blend on high speed for 30–40 seconds. Add sugar to taste and let stand 3 hours.

Soften 2 envelopes plain gelatin in ½ cup cold water and dissolve over hot water. Stir into the strawberry purée and chill. When it starts to thicken fold in 2 cups heavy cream whipped, turn into a mold, and chill for several hours. Unmold and garnish with whole berries. *Serves 6–8.*

STRAWBERRIES OR RASPBERRIES IN DUBONNET

THE flavor of this dessert comes from the Dubonnet wine, which is rapidly becoming a great favorite with Americans. Wash and stem or hull a quart of either strawberries or raspberries and place them in a deep bowl. Sugar them lightly and pour over ⅔ cup of Dubonnet. Twist over the bowl 3 thin slices of lemon and drop one slice into the bowl until serving time. Chill the bowl of berries at least 1 hour and serve in clear glass or crystal serving dishes. *Serves 6.*

STRAWBERRY-MELON CUP

4 cups cantaloupe balls
2 cups sliced fresh strawberries
2 tablespoons sugar

¼ cup sherry
6 sprigs fresh mint

COMBINE all but the mint and chill thoroughly. Garnish each serving with a sprig of mint. *Serves 6.*

FRUIT CUP WITH CHAMPAGNE

16-ounce package frozen whole strawberries thawed
12-ounce package frozen sliced peaches thawed

13¼-ounce can frozen pineapple chunks
¼ cup peach brandy
1 bottle well-chilled champagne

COMBINE the fruits, stir the brandy in, and refrigerate at least 2 hours. Spoon into large glases and pour champagne over at serving time. *Serves 6.*

MARY ANNE'S STRAWBERRIES ROMANOV

CHILL for an hour 1 quart strawberries washed and hulled, 1 cup sugar, 2 ounces Curaçao liqueur, and 2 ounces brandy. Soften 1 pint vanilla ice cream and fold the strawberries in. Then fold in 1 pint cream whipped stiff. Serve in parfait glasses.

Without the liquor this is a well-known dessert, but it is surely enhanced with the liquor as indicated here. *Serves 6.*

FROZEN DESSERTS

ALMOND-CREAM FREEZE

¼ cup toasted slivered or sliced
   almonds
⅓ cup sugar
2 tablespoons water

2 tablespoons dry sherry
3 egg yolks
1 cup heavy cream whipped

1. Put almonds in blender about 8-10 seconds to grind fine.
2. Boil sugar and water in a small saucepan 3 minutes.
3. Put sherry and egg yolks in blender and start the motor at high speed. Remove the center piece in the cover and pour in the syrup very slowly, with the motor running.
4. Turn off the motor and fold the blender contents into the whipped cream.
5. Spoon into custard cups and sprinkle with the almonds. Set on a tray, cover with foil, and freeze 2–3 hours, or until frozen. *Serves 8.*

HAWAIIAN PUNCH ICE CREAM PIE

2 cups graham cracker crumbs
¼ cup sugar
½ cup melted butter or margarine

2 quarts vanilla ice cream softened
6 tablespoons frozen Hawaiian
   Punch thawed

1. Combine the graham cracker crumbs, sugar, and butter well, and press into 2 well-greased 9" x 5" x 3" loaf pans, extending the crumb mixture about 2 inches up the sides of the pans. Or use graham cracker piecrust mix. Chill.
2. Swirl the Hawaiian Punch through the softened ice cream just enough to make streaks all through it. Press into the crumb-lined pans and freeze again. *Serves 8–10.*

ICE CREAM BALLS

HAVE soup plates of shredded coconut, crumbled macaroons, chocolate shot, salted peanuts coarsely chopped, walnuts chopped fine, etc. Drop scoops of various kinds of ice cream into the plates, roll them around in that coating, and pile the coated balls on a serving plate. Wrap the plate of ice cream balls with foil or wax paper and put in freezer until serving time. Or have the plates of coatings ready and prepare the balls just at serving time. If desired, chocolate sauce can be poured over each serving.

ICE CREAM CAKE

1 quart strawberry ice cream
1 quart lemon sherbet

1 quart vanilla ice cream melted
3 cups heavy cream whipped

FILL a 9-inch tube pan with scoops of strawberry ice cream and lemon sherbet. Freeze until firm. Pour the melted vanilla ice cream over the ice cream balls to fill in all the spaces. Freeze. When frozen unmold on a serving plate and frost all over with the whipped cream. Return to freezer until serving time. *Serves 10–12.*

ICE CREAM SOUFFLÉ WITH GRAND MARNIER SAUCE

1 quart vanilla ice cream
8 almond macaroons crumbled
¼ cup Grand Marnier liqueur
¾ cup heavy cream whipped

Sauce
1 quart fresh strawberries washed
  and hulled
½ cup sugar
2 tablespoons Grand Marnier

1. Let the ice cream stand in the refrigerator an hour to soften a little.
2. In a bowl blend the softened ice cream with the macaroon crumbs, Grand Marnier, and whipped cream. Freeze in refrigerator tray.
3. Just before serving time combine the well-drained berries with the sugar and cook over low heat until the sugar dissolves and the berries are hot and have just begun to soften. Remove from the heat and stir in the Grand Marnier.
4. Pour the hot sauce over the ice cream and serve at once. *Serves 6.*

CRÈME DE CACAO SAUCE FOR ICE CREAM

GRATE 6 squares of dark sweet chocolate into a small heavy saucepan. Add 6 tablespoons cold coffee and stir over low heat until smooth and velvety. Stir in 1 tablespoon crème de cacao and serve hot over coffee ice cream.

CRÈME DE MENTHE ICE CREAM WITH PEARS AND CHOCOLATE SAUCE

2 quarts vanilla ice cream softened a little
¼ cup green crème de menthe liqueur

1-pound-13-ounce can pears well drained
1 cup chocolate syrup

1. Put the ice cream in a large bowl and stir it up. Add the crème de menthe and stir it in just enough to make green streaks through the ice cream. Refreeze until firm and make scoops of it. Lay them on a platter, cover, and keep frozen until ready to put the dessert together.
2. Put the pear halves in a large shallow serving plate, cut side up. When ready to serve put a scoop of the crème de menthe ice cream in each pear and pour chocolate sauce over. *Serves 8.*

BOMBE GLACÉE

LINE a decorative mold or a melon mold with slightly softened ice cream to a depth of 1–1½ inches. Fill the center with a contrasting ice cream or a fruit ice, cover with more of the original ice cream, fold foil over the top, and freeze. Good combinations are chocolate with pistachio, strawberry with pistachio, rum raisin with pineapple or mint sherbet, strawberry with lemon sherbet, etc. Serve with butterscotch or chocolate sauce or with a sweet liqueur.

FROZEN LEMON CUSTARD

3 tablespoons lemon juice
½ teaspoon grated lemon rind
⅓ cup sugar
Pinch salt

1 egg separated
⅓ cup water
⅓ cup instant nonfat dry milk
¼ cup graham-cracker crumbs

1. Mix the lemon juice and rind, sugar, salt, and yolk of egg.
2. Put in a bowl the egg white, water, and dry milk and beat until the mixture stands in peaks. Gradually beat in the lemon mixture.
3. Put in 1-quart freezer tray, sprinkle the crumbs on top, and freeze without stirring until firm. *Serves 4.*

FROZEN LIME PIE

Pie Shell

1½ cups graham-cracker crumbs
¼ cup confectioners' sugar
¼ teaspoon cinnamon
¼ cup melted butter or margarine

Filling

½ cup sugar
2 eggs beaten until thick

½ cup light corn syrup
1 cup cream or top milk
1 cup milk
⅓ cup lime juice
1 teaspoon grated lime rind
Green vegetable coloring (optional)

1. Make the shell first. Blend all the ingredients together and press onto the bottom and sides of a buttered pie plate. Reserve ¼ cup for later use. Put the shell in the freezing unit while the filling is being prepared. Or use graham cracker piecrust mix for the shell.
2. Beat the sugar gradually into the eggs. When they are thick and lemon-colored stir in the remaining ingredients. The appearance of the pie will be improved if you also add a couple of drops of green vegetable coloring.
3. Pour the mixture into a freezer tray and freeze until almost hard.
4. Scrape the ice cream into a chilled bowl and beat until smooth but not melted.
5. Pour into the chilled shell, top with the reserved crumbs, and freeze until firm. *Serves 6–8.*

172

MINT SUNDAES

8 one-inch chocolate-covered mint   1 tablespoon water
   patties   1 cup heavy cream

MELT mints in top of double boiler over boiling water. Add water and stir until smooth. Cool slightly and then stir into cream. Beat until stiff and serve over ice cream. *Serves 4.*

DIFFERENT PEACH MELBA

SPREAD slightly softened vanilla ice cream in a freezer tray, freeze it hard, and spread a layer of slightly softened raspberry ice or sherbet over it. Leave in freezer until serving time. When cut into serving portions, lay a half peach, fresh and peeled, or canned, on each serving, cut side down. Serve with Melba sauce poured over.

PEPPERMINT-STICK PARFAIT

½ cup sugar   1⅔ cups chilled evaporated milk
½ cup water   ½ cup finely crushed peppermint-
⅛ teaspoon salt   stick candy
2 egg whites

1. Cook the sugar and water together to 230°F., or until the syrup spins a thread.
2. Add salt to egg whites and beat until stiff but not dry.
3. Pour the hot syrup slowly into the egg whites, beating constantly. Chill.
4. Whip evaporated milk very stiff. Fold in egg whites and candy. Freeze until firm. *Serves 6.*

QUICK ICE-CREAM CAKE

8-inch sponge cake, fairly thick
1 pint vanilla ice cream somewhat
  softened

1 pint raspberry sherbet
  somewhat softened
1½ cups heavy cream whipped and
  sweetened

1. Slit the cake into 2 layers and spread the ice cream over the bottom layer as smoothly as possible.
2. Spread the raspberry sherbet over the ice cream. Put on the second layer of cake.
3. Frost the top and sides with the whipped cream and put in the freezer 2–3 hours. Serve with raspberry sauce (*see Index*). *Serves 8–10.*

STRAWBERRY ICE-CREAM PIE

Baked deep 8-inch pie shell
1 quart strawberry ice cream
  somewhat softened
3 egg whites

¼ teaspoon salt
¾ teaspoon cream of tartar
6 tablespoons sugar
1 teaspoon vanilla

THIS is really a form of baked Alaska, and it is just as good and just as spectacular as that popular dessert, and a little easier to make.
1. Pack the ice cream firmly in the pie shell and refreeze at once.
2. Beat the egg whites with the salt until almost stiff. Add the cream of tartar and then gradually beat in the sugar until the meringue is very stiff. Stir in the vanilla.
3. Spread the meringue over the ice cream carefully, making sure there are no gaps or holes, and that the meringue is in contact with the edge of the pie shell all around.
4. Bake in a hot oven, 450°, 4–5 minutes, or until the meringue is a delicate brown. Serve at once. *Serves 6.*

FROZEN PEACH-MACAROON TORTE

2 cups mashed peaches
1 cup sugar (more if needed)
1 tablespoon lemon juice

1 cup heavy cream whipped
1 cup coarse almond macaroon
  crumbs

1. Mix the peaches, sugar, and lemon juice. Fold in the whipped cream.
2. Spread half of the crumbs on the bottom of a 1-quart refrigerator tray, add the peach mixture, and top with the rest of the crumbs. Freeze until firm, 4–6 hours. *Serves 6–8.*

PIES

BLUEBERRY CREAM PIE

8-ounce package cream cheese
  softened
2 tablespoons milk
2-ounce package dessert topping
  mix

1 pound 5-ounce can blueberry pie
  filling
9-inch-graham-cracker crumb crust
  (see *Index*)

BEAT together the cheese and milk. Prepare the dessert topping mix according to instructions on package. Fold into the cheese and turn into the crust. Spoon the blueberry filling on top and chill until firm. *Serves 6–8.*

CHERRY CREAM CHEESE PIE

8-ounce package cream cheese
softened
15-ounce can sweetened condensed
milk
⅓ cup fresh lemon juice
1 teaspoon vanilla
Graham-cracker-crumb (see
Index) or baked 9-inch pie
shell

2 tablespoons sugar
2 teaspoons cornstarch
½ cup cherry juice
Few drops red food coloring
1-pound-6-ounce can sour
cherry pie filling

1. Beat the cheese until fluffy and gradually stir in the milk, lemon juice, and vanilla. Pour into the crust and chill 2–3 hours.
2. Blend the sugar and cornstarch. Stir in the ½ cup juice of the canned cherries and cook until clear and thick, stirring constantly.
3. Add a little red food coloring to deepen the color, and stir in a cup of the pie filling. Cool.
4. Pour the cherry glaze on top of the cream filling in the pie shell and chill again before serving. *Serves 6–8.*

SPECIAL LEMON MERINGUE PIE

Juice and grated rind of 1 lemon
1 cup water
1 cup sugar
4 eggs separated

1 heaping tablespoon cornstarch
8-inch baked pie shell
½ teaspoon vanilla

1. Put the lemon juice and rind, water, and ¾ cup of the sugar in a small saucepan and boil a few minutes.
2. Beat the egg yolks well, stir in the cornstarch, and gradually blend in the lemon syrup. Cook until thick and smooth.
3. Cool the filling and then fold in 2 of the egg whites beaten until stiff but not dry. Spread in the pie shell.
4. Beat the remaining 2 egg whites until stiff but not dry and gradually beat in the remaining ¼ cup of sugar. Stir in the vanilla and spread the meringue on top of the pie. Bake 15 minutes in a slow oven, 275°, or until delicately browned. *Serves 6.*

NESSELRODE CHIFFON PIE

1 envelope plain gelatin
⅔ cup sugar
⅛ teaspoon salt
3 eggs separated
1¼ cups milk
1 cup heavy cream

3 tablespoons rum or sherry, or
2 teaspoons rum flavoring
1 tablespoon chopped maraschino
cherries
9-inch baked pie shell
Shaved bitter chocolate

1. In the top of a double boiler mix the gelatin, ⅓ cup of the sugar, and the salt.
2. Beat the egg yolks, milk, and cream together and stir into the gelatin-sugar mixture. Cook over boiling water, stirring, until the gelatin and sugar are both dissolved. Remove from the heat and stir in the rum.
3. Chill the mixture until it mounds when dropped from a spoon.
4. Beat the egg whites until stiff but not dry and beat in gradually the remaining ⅓ cup of sugar.
5. Gently combine the egg whites, the gelatin mixture, and the cherries. Turn into the baked pie shell and grate chocolate quite thickly over the top. Chill. *Serves 6.*

STRAWBERRY PIE

1 quart fresh strawberries washed
and hulled
Baked 9-inch pie shell

3 eggs separated
½ cup sugar
½ cup flour

1. Drain the strawberries well and arrange them in the baked pie shell.
2. Beat the egg yolks until light and gradually beat in the sugar. Add the flour and beat until smooth.
3. Beat the egg whites until stiff but not dry and fold into the yolk mixture.
4. Pour over the berries and bake 8 minutes at 375°, and then at 325° until golden brown. Serve slightly warm with sweetened whipped cream. *Serves 6.*

PEACH PIE

¼ cup sugar
¼ cup light brown sugar
2 tablespoons cornstarch
½ teaspoon salt
Cinnamon
2 cups dairy sour cream

¼ cup honey
⅛ teaspoon almond extract
2 egg yolks beaten
Pastry for 10-inch pie
4-5 cups sliced peaches
2 tablespoons brown sugar

1. Roll out pastry for the lower crust, fit in pie plate, and bake in a hot oven, 400°, 8–10 minutes. Cool.
2. Put in the top of a double boiler the sugar, ¼ cup brown sugar, cornstarch, salt, a pinch of cinnamon, 1½ cups of the sour cream, honey, almond extract, and egg yolks. Cook over hot but not boiling water until thickened, stirring frequently. Cool.
3. Drain the sliced peaches thoroughly and fold them into the custard. Turn into the shell.
4. Roll out pastry for the top crust, cut into strips, and make a latticed top for the pie.
5. Bake the pie 15 minutes in a hot oven, 450°, reduce the heat to 350°, and continue to bake until the crust is golden. Cool.
6. Before serving, mix the remaining ½ cup sour cream with the 2 tablespoons brown sugar and a pinch of cinnamon and spread over the pie. *Serves 10–12.*

MOLDED DESSERTS

JELLIED AMBROSIA

1 envelope plain gelatin
¼ cup cold water
¼ cup boiling water
¼ cup sugar
1¼ cups orange juice

1 tablespoon lemon juice
2 large oranges sectioned (skin sections)
1 large banana sliced
3 tablespoons flaked coconut

1. Sprinkle the gelatin on cold water and dissolve in boiling water.
2. Stir in the sugar, orange juice, and lemon juice. Chill until syrupy.

3. Fold the oranges, banana, and coconut into the gelatin mixture and chill until firm. *Serves 4.*

COLD APRICOT SOUFFLÉ

4 eggs plus 3 yolks
½ cup sugar
1 cup thick stewed apricots
mashed or apricot marmalade

1 tablespoon cognac (optional)
½ cup heavy cream whipped
2 tablespoons plain gelatin
2 tablespoons lemon juice

1. Beat the eggs and extra yolks with the sugar until thick and pale.
2. Stir in the apricots, cognac, cream, and gelatin dissolved in the lemon juice over low heat.
3. Pour into a buttered soufflé dish and chill at least 2–3 hours. Garnish with sweetened whipped cream. *Serves 6.*

APRICOT BAVARIAN ANGEL

1 tablespoon plain gelatin
¼ cup orange juice
½ cup sugar
1 cup apricot purée or apricot
preserves mashed

1 tablespoon lemon juice
Pinch salt
1 cup heavy cream whipped
1 small angel food cake

1. Soften gelatin in orange juice and dissolve over hot water, stirring until dissolved.
2. Remove the orange juice from the heat and stir in the sugar, apricot purée, lemon juice, and salt. Chill until thick, about 15–20 minutes.
3. Beat until frothy and fold in whipped cream.
4. Slice the angel food cake into 3 layers crosswise and spread the Bavarian mixture between the layers and also on the top and sides of the cake. Chill until firm.

Note: A pleasant variation of this dessert is to use 2 packages of ladyfingers instead of the angel food. For extra flavor dip the split ladyfingers lightly into light rum or apricot cordial. *Serves 8–10.*

AVOCADO DESSERT MOLD

2 ripe avocados peeled and cut up
Juice of 2 lemons
Juice of 4 oranges
¾ cup honey
1 cup light cream
Few drops green vegetable
coloring
¼ teaspoon almond extract
¼ cup Cointreau or Curaçao
(optional)

2 tablespoons plain gelatin
¼ cup cold water
4 egg whites
1 cup confectioners' sugar
½ cup heavy cream
2 tablespoons sugar
1 tablespoon same liqueur used
above

1. Mash the avocados to a smooth pulp or put them in a blender 30–40 seconds.
2. Stir into the avocados the fruit juices, honey, light cream, food coloring to your liking, almond extract, and liqueur if you use it.
3. Soften the gelatin in cold water and dissolve it over hot water. Stir into the avocado mixture.
4. Beat the egg whites until stiff but not dry, gradually stirring in the confectioners' sugar.
5. Fold the avocado mixture into the egg whites gently and pour into a mold rinsed out in cold water.
6. Unmold on a chilled platter at serving time and pour over the mold the heavy cream beaten until stiff, and with the sugar and liqueur added, if used. *Serves 8–10.*

BING CHERRY MOLD

1 pound-4-ounce can pitted Bing
cherries

1 package raspberry-flavored
gelatin
Toasted almonds

1. Drain the juice from the cherries and add enough water to it to make 2 cups liquid.
2. Heat the liquid and stir the raspberry gelatin into it until dissolved.

180

Pour half of this gelatin into a loaf pan 8½" x 4½" x 2½". Chill until it begins to thicken.

3. Split the almonds and put ½ almond into each cherry. Arrange the cherries on top of the gelatin, top with the rest of the gelatin mixture, and chill until firm. Unmold and serve with sweetened whipped cream or cream cheese beaten until fluffy with a little cream. *Serves 8.*

BLACK CHERRY MOLD

2 cans pitted black cherries
drained (save juice)
2 tablespoons gelatin
½ cup cold cherry juice

3 cups hot cherry juice
1 cup dry red wine
½ pound cream cheese softened
Pineapple juice

1. Arrange the drained cherries in a ring mold.
2. Sprinkle gelatin on the cold cherry juice, add to hot cherry juice, and stir until gelatin is dissolved. Stir in the wine and pour over cherries in the mold. Chill until firm.
3. Beat the cream cheese until soft and fluffy and blend in the pineapple juice.
4. Unmold the cherry ring on a chilled plate and pile the cream cheese sauce in the center. *Serves 6–8.*

RAINBOW ROOM CHOCOLATE MOUSSE FOR A PARTY

8 ounces sweet chocolate
8 ounces bitter chocolate
¾ cup plus 2 tablespoons sugar

5 egg whites beaten until stiff
4 cups heavy cream whipped

1. In the top of a double boiler, over simmering water, melt the chocolates.
2. Beat the sugar into the egg whites.
3. Combine the egg white and chocolate mixtures and fold in the whipped cream. Turn into a large mold and chill several hours, or until firm.
4. Turn out on a chilled platter and decorate with sweetened whipped cream. *Serves 15–20.*

CANTALOUPE BANANA

2 tablespoons confectioners' sugar
1 egg white slightly beaten
⅓ cup light cream scalded
1 tablespoon plain gelatin
¼ cup cold water
⅔ cup sugar

1 ripe cantaloupe, seeded,
    peeled, and mashed
⅓ cup mashed banana
½ tablespoon lemon juice
1¾ cups heavy cream whipped
12 ladyfingers

1. Add the confectioners' sugar to the beaten egg white and gradually beat in the hot cream. Cook over hot water until it thickens. Stir in the gelatin, which has been sprinkled over the cold water, and keep stirring until the gelatin is dissolved.
2. Add the ⅔ cup sugar, the cantaloupe, the banana, and the lemon juice. Blend well and chill until it begins to set.
3. Fold in the whipped cream and pour into a melon-shaped mold which has been lined with split ladyfingers.
4. Unmold on a chilled dessert plate. *Serves 8–10.*

JELLIED SUMMER FRUIT

2 envelopes plain gelatin
2¾ cups cold water
⅔ cup sugar
⅛ teaspoon salt
½ cup lime or lemon juice

4 cups mixed fresh fruit well
    drained (halved peaches, cut
    pears, seeded or seedless grapes,
    raspberries, blueberries, etc.)

1. Sprinkle gelatin over 1 cup of the water and place over low heat. Add sugar and salt and stir until dissolved. Add remaining 1¾ cups water and lime or lemon juice. Chill until syrupy.
2. Arrange some of the fruit on the bottom of a mold rinsed out in cold water and spoon enough of the gelatin mixture over it to cover. Chill until almost firm. At the same time chill the remaining gelatin until it begins to thicken.
3. Fold the remaining fruit into the chilled gelatin mixture and pour over the mold. Chill until firm.
4. Unmold on chilled platter and serve with sweetened whipped cream or cream cheese beaten until fluffy with a little cream. *Serves 10–12.*

EASY MOLDED FRUIT SALAD DESSERT

2 cups canned fruit cocktail
drained (save syrup)
¾ cup water or syrup from fruit
cocktail
2 tablespoons plain gelatin
1⅔ cups pineapple tidbits drained

¼ cup lemon juice
1 cup chopped nuts
¼ cup maraschino cherries chopped
1 cup evaporated milk
2 tablespoons lemon juice

1. Heat the syrup or water to boiling and pour over the gelatin. Stir until dissolved and chill until thickened to the consistency of raw egg whites.
2. Stir in fruit-cocktail fruit, pineapple, the ¼ cup lemon juice, nuts, and maraschino cherries.
3. Chill the evaporated milk in a freezer tray until crystals begin to form around the edges. Scrape into a bowl and beat until stiff. Add the 2 tablespoons lemon juice and whip about 2 minutes more, until very stiff.
4. Fold the milk mixture into the gelatin mixture, pour into a mold, and chill until firm, about 2 hours. *Serves 6–8.*

HAWAIIAN SNOW

1 envelope plain gelatin
½ cup sugar
⅛ teaspoon salt

1 cup water
6-ounce can frozen Hawaiian Punch
2 unbeaten egg whites

1. Mix the gelatin, sugar, and salt, and add ½ cup of the water. Place over low heat, stirring constantly until gelatin is dissolved. Remove from the heat and stir in the other ½ cup of water and the frozen Hawaiian Punch. Stir until the punch is melted and chill until the consistency of raw egg whites.
2. Add the unbeaten whites to the chilled liquid and beat until it begins to hold its shape. Spoon into dessert dishes and chill. *Serves 6–7.*

LEMON CLOUD

1 envelope plain gelatin
½ cup cold water
1 cup sugar

5 eggs separated
½ cup lemon juice
1 teaspoon grated lemon rind

1. Sprinkle the gelatin over the water. Add ¼ cup of the sugar and stir over low heat until both the gelatin and the sugar are dissolved. Remove from heat.
2. Beat the egg yolks with the lemon juice and stir in thoroughly the gelatin mixture and lemon rind. Chill to the consistency of raw egg whites.
3. Beat the egg whites until stiff but not dry and gradually beat in the remaining ¾ cup sugar.
4. Combine the 2 mixtures gently but thoroughly, pour into a mold, and chill until firm. Unmold on a chilled plate and serve with sweetened whipped cream. *Serves 8.*

LIME-MINT GELATIN

1 envelope plain gelatin
½ cup cold water
1 tablespoon fresh mint leaves
   chopped fine

⅓ cup sugar
¼ cup lime juice
1¼ cups canned pineapple juice
Green food coloring

1. Sprinkle the gelatin over the water in a small saucepan and dissolve over low heat. Stir in the mint and sugar and keep stirring until both the gelatin and the sugar are dissolved. Let stand 10–15 minutes.
2. Stir in the lime and pineapple juices, and add green food coloring, a drop or two at a time, to color it a delicate mint green.
3. Turn into a mold rinsed out with cold water and chill until set. Serve with a dab of whipped cream, slightly sweetened. *Serves 4.*

PEACH CREAM

1 cup sugar
⅓ cup sherry
¼ cup light rum
4 eggs separated
Juice of 1 lemon
Pinch salt

Pinch grated nutmeg
1 tablespoon plain gelatin
¼ cup sherry
½ cup dairy sour cream
2 sliced peaches

1. In the top of a double boiler stir together the sugar, ⅓ cup sherry, rum, egg yolks, lemon juice, salt, and nutmeg. Cook over boiling water until the consistency of heavy cream, stirring constantly. Remove from the heat and stir in the gelatin softened in the ¼ cup sherry. Stir until dissolved. Cool.
2. Put ½ cup of this custard mixture into a blender with the sour cream and peaches. Blend well, combine with the rest of the custard and chill until the mixture is the consistency of raw egg whites.
3. Beat the egg whites until they are stiff but not dry and fold into the chilled custard mixture. Pour into a medium mold and chill at least 4 hours, or until firm. Garnish with fresh peach slices when serving. *Serves 8.*

FRESH PEACH BAVARIAN

1½ cups chopped fresh peaches
2 tablespoons lemon juice
¼ teaspoon salt
⅔ cup sugar
1½ tablespoons plain gelatin

½ cup cold water
1 cup heavy cream whipped
1 teaspoon vanilla
½ teaspoon almond extract

1. Combine the peaches, lemon juice, salt, and sugar, and let stand 1 hour.
2. Sprinkle the gelatin over the cold water and dissolve it over low heat. Stir it into the peach mixture and chill until it begins to thicken.
3. Fold in the whipped cream and flavorings. Pour into one large mold rinsed in cold water or into 8 individual molds. Chill several hours.
4. Unmold on a chilled dessert plate and serve with more fresh sliced peaches and/or whipped cream. *Serves 8.*

RASPBERRY CHARLOTTE

1 envelope plain gelatin	1 cup heavy cream whipped
2 tablespoons cold water	8 ladyfingers split
½ cup crushed raspberries	1 pint raspberries
⅓ cup sugar	1 cup sugar
2 tablespoons lemon juice	⅓ cup water
Pinch salt	

1. Soften the gelatin in cold water and dissolve over boiling water. Stir in the crushed raspberries, sugar, lemon juice, and salt, and stir until the sugar is dissolved. Fold in whipped cream. Chill until almost set.
2. Arrange the ladyfingers around a 1½-quart mold (spread them with a little raspberry jam or jelly if you like). Fill the mold with the gelatin-cream mixture and chill until firm.
3. Serve the charlotte with raspberry purée, which is made by putting the pint of raspberries through a fine sieve or food mill, and stirring into this purée a syrup made by boiling the cup of sugar and ⅓ cup of water until the consistency of a thin syrup. Cool before serving. *Serves 4–6.*

RASPBERRY CREAM

FORCE 1½ quarts raspberries through a sieve or food mill, sweeten to taste, and let stand 3–4 hours. Soften 2 envelopes plain gelatin in ½ cup cold water and dissolve over low heat, stirring until well dissolved. Add to the purée and chill until it begins to set. Fold in 1 pint cream whipped until stiff and chill at least 2 hours longer. Unmold and garnish with a few fresh ripe raspberries. *Serves 6–8.*

186

STRAWBERRY FLUFF

1 cup sugar	¼ cup cold water
2 cups strawberries crushed	2 egg whites
1½ tablespoons plain gelatin	Juice of ½ lemon

1. Stir ½ cup of the sugar into the berries and cook them about 10 minutes over low heat.
2. Sprinkle the gelatin over the water and add to the berries, stirring until dissolved. Chill.
3. When the berry mixture begins to thicken, stir in the egg whites beaten with the remaining ½ cup sugar and the lemon juice. Pour into a mold which has been rinsed in cold water and chill until set.
4. Unmold on a chilled dessert plate and garnish with more fresh strawberries. *Serves 4.*

INDEX

192

194

198

200

THE MOST COMMON HERBS

HERBS	SOUPS	EGGS	CHEESE	FISH
BASIL *Leaves* *used* *Annual*	Tomato and others	Omelets Stuffed eggs	Cottage cheese and others	In court bouillon Mackerel Fish sauces
BAY LEAF *Dried* *leaf of bay* *tree*	Fish Tomato stock		Cottage cheese	Boiled
CARAWAY *Biennial* *Seeds* *used*	Vegetable stock		Cream cheese and others	
CHERVIL *Annual* *Leaves* *used*	Asparagus Chicken Spinach Creamed	Any egg dish	Any cheese dish	Broiled Sauces
CHIVES *Perennial* *Stems* *used*	Bean Pea Vichyssoise	Omelets	Cottage cheese Cream cheese	
DILL *Annual* *Leaves* *and seeds* *used*		Many egg dishes	Many cheese dishes	Broiled fish Shrimp
MARJORAM *Perennial* *Leaf* *used*	All stock soups Potato	Almost all	Many cheese dishes	All fish All stuffings All sauces
ORÉGANO *Perennial* *Leaf* *used*			Fresh in cream cheese	
PARSLEY *Annual* *Leaf* *used*	All soups	Omelets Scrambled eggs	Many	Sauces Marinades
ROSEMARY *Perennial* *Leaf* *used*	Many meat base soups Many poultry base soups	Some egg dishes		
SAGE *Perennial* *Leaf* *used*	Most		Fresh in cottage cheese	Baked
TARRAGON *Perennial* *Leaf* *used*	Potato Tomato	Omelets Many egg dishes	Many cheese dishes	Broiled Salmon Tartar sauce Fish sauces
THYME *Perennial* *Leaf* *used*	All stock soups	Many egg dishes	Some cheese dishes	Chowders Fried fish